THE NETWORK EFFECT

"Stories from The Inside Circle"

Scott Manthorne

The Network Effect

CONTENTS

ENDORSEMENTS

"I have had the pleasure of knowing Scott Manthorne for many years now, and I can confidently say that he is a trusted resource and a truly competent individual. What sets Scott apart is his unwavering character, integrity, and honesty, which are the key ingredients that make him stand out. Scott always conducts himself with the highest ethical standards and is dedicated to providing his best in all aspects of his life, be it personal or professional. I have seen Scott consistently demonstrate his commitment to excellence and his ability to always do the right thing, no matter the circumstances. He is a man of his word and always follows through on his promises. In short, Scott is someone you can always count on, and I wholeheartedly endorse him as a man of impeccable character and exceptional abilities." – **Aaron Walker**, *Founder and CEO of View from the Top*

Networking like anything else is a process. I was a business partner of Scott Manthorne's for over a decade. The networking process that he uses employs techniques that are extraordinarily effective. He is simply the most knowledgeable person I know in the area of networking. - **Alan Pavlosky**, *Owner Administrator at The Good Earth School*

Scott has the ability to assemble the right people that need to connect with each other. At those meetings, he has the ability to inject comfortable energy to motivate the participants to engage. - **Andy Andrus,** *Entrepreneur, Consultant and Philanthropist*

I dislike the word "networking " but Scott is one of the best relationship builders I know. He's leveraged his decades of meeting exceptional people and establishing genuine connections to give us a chance to learn about great leadership from some amazing leaders. – **Charles Baker,** *Co-Chair, Entertainment, Sports and Media Group, Sidley*

Over the years I've been a part of just about every networking group/mastermind you can think of. I've yet to experience another individual more connected and willing to help than Scott. He has a unique ability to identify the connection points between two parties and make an introduction that is mutually beneficial. My network has dramatically improved since bumping into Scott. He's become a great resource for my endeavors, but more importantly he's become a great friend. – **Cody Harvey**, *Co-Founder and CEO, Breakout App*

There are few things more rewarding in business than surrounding yourself with people who support you as you pursue your potential. The Network Effect is a great guide on how to connect with the right people to take your career to the next level. - **David Meltzer,** *Co-founder of Sports 1 Marketing, best-selling author, and top business coach*

I am pleased that Scott took the initiative to do the interviews and capture the stories to create The Network Effect. He is the right guy to dispel the myths and elevate what true networking is all about. His own career in building strategic relationships, communities of aligned people and facilitating value-added engagement is a model that should guide readers in building the foundation for their own rewarding professional networks. - **Danny Hughes**, *Co-Founder and Partner, LOHAS Advisors*

When I first met Scott Manthorne, I had never heard of a "Connector." But as I began to know him, I found he had nailed the secret of how making strategic connections can not only help you in business, but more importantly, impact people's lives. In "The Network Effect," he shows you how the people he has "connected" have used the strategies to impact thousands of lives! – **Dave Sanderson**, *International Keynote Speaker*

"Network" should be Scott's middle name. Actually, I wouldn't be surprised if it was listed that way on his birth certificate. Scott knows better than anyone I've met that having a network means building strategic connections and personally connecting those individuals on an even more strategic basis, so that everyone thrives. Asking "Who can I introduce you to?" and "How can I help you right now?" is like breathing to him. He's opened doors and taught me lessons great and small over the years, and I strive to pay it forward in my daily interactions. No doubt this book will help you, too. - **Diane Byrne**, *Founder and Editor of MegaYachtNews.com*

Scott masters the fine art of connecting deeply with people to build high-quality human and business relations. Scott deploys genuine efforts to support and connect the members of his community. A rare quality in today's world. I am honored by his friendship and business-partnership. - **Enzo di Taranto**, *Climate Finance, Celebrity Diplomacy, Global Campaigns*

"Scott wrote the book on networking." I used to say that figuratively, but now I can say it literally! I have benefitted from being part of his ridiculously large network countless times over the past dozen years and I'll be the first in line to read how the master does it! - **Greg Antonioli**, *Owner/President, First Call Residential*

Scott has a real talent for cutting through the noise to find common and unique interests that bring people together. His strategic acumen and candid delivery style makes for dynamic, efficient, and impactful connections. Our organization earned major media coverage, new venture capital connections and highly qualified business prospects because of Scott's programs and network. - **Jason Ford**, *President at Frisco Economic Development Corporation*

Scott has an amazingly varied, curated network of solid, incredible C-level professionals. He has been beyond helpful with his connections, insights and ability to introduce the right people in the right way. Thank you, Scott! - **Jeff Turk**, *Co-Founder, Mount Hydra Biotech*

I've known Scott for many years and what always struck me is how he continually evolves and finds new ways to bring value to his friends and associates. It's hard to do over and over again, but he's mastered that skill. - **Jeffrey Menaged**, *Founder and CEO at Chief Executive Air*

Scott Manthorne is a true force multiplier. Hard to name anyone who adds more value to anyone's personal network. And that's because he leads with gratitude and attracts the right positive energy into his circle. - **John Brenkus**, *Founder and CEO of BrinxTV*

Scott is a networking guru who is genuine about sharing his tactics with others. Scott does a great job of storytelling to get across key learnings about business development. Scott is the go-to expert on networking and I know this book can help all walks of life on their journey to expand their network. – **Josh Folds**, *Head of Small Business, Small Business Banking, Merchant Services and SBA at First Horizon Bank*

The rooms Scott has curated through Roundtable and zoom have expanded my network beyond my wildest imagination and created some friendships and business relationships that have lasted years. I'm grateful to be in his network. - **LaVonne Idlette**, *Passionate Wealth Strategist for Athletes and Professionals*

Scott has been a master connector and has helped many individuals and businesses with powerful business relationships. - **Luciane Serifovic**, *CEO and Founder, Luxian International Realty*

Scott's decades of networking experience prove him not only to be a winner but to be the best connector in the business! – **MJ Pedone**, *President and Founder, Indra Public Relations*

Scott is truly a people's super-connector. His ability to listen deeply and connect with people is powerful and he shares that gift so freely with those he meets. – **Maayan Gordon**, *Founder, Maayan Gordon Media*

Scott is the master connector.... and a connector for good. He focuses on making the best connection for both/all parties and is more interested in the outcomes for business and life than what he gets in return. - **Marissa Fayer**, *Non-profit CEO of HERhealthEQ; Medical Device CEO of DeepLook Medical; Partner at Goodess Gaia Ventures; TEDx speaker*

Scott is an amazing and gifted networker and advisor. It was due to his input and feedback that my business partner and I ended up helping out in the PPE space early during the pandemic. We are still working in that space as the need arises and doing so ethically and with good partners. Scott has introduced many great contacts to me over the years and I consider him one of the most valuable members of my network. - **Mary Kurek**, *Founder and President, Frontrunners Development, Inc.*

Scott Manthorne is the best networker I have ever experienced. In my long legal career. For 11 years I served as an Executive Partner of a 1300-person law firm and was constantly trying to help lawyers find clients. Professionals who don't understand the results of networking will pay professionally for their lack of understanding. I recommend they read The Network Effect. - **Michael Moore**, *CEO, Moore and Company, P.A.*

I met Scott many years ago and have become close friends. Scott has an uncanny ability to navigate and develop high-level relationships. He's compiled what I think will become a must read. I know my copy will be dogeared, highlighted and written in so please don't ask to borrow it because I'll most likely be re-reading it also. Congratulations on this important and incredible book! - **Scott MacGregor**, *Founder and CEO of SomethingNew LLC, Founder and CEO of The Outlier Project, 5x author, 8x winner of the American Business Award for Innovation*

For most of us, connecting the way Scott Manthorne seems impossible. Fortunately, this generous book lays open the secrets to his success! -- **Seth Buechley**, *Executive Chairman at Cathedral*

Scott spent time understanding my professional aspirations over 15 years ago and without hesitation, he opened his "Rolodex" to make a match of my skills with other corporate entities looking for a speaker/wellness influencer. As a result, I had the opportunity to fly the world over speaking, teaching and training. After those first introductions rolled a tsunami of positive launches in my career. Those connections have translated into a lifetime of positive business networking and have also taught me the immense value of intentional networking. The principles I learned from Scott I was also able to teach to my own children, and as young adults they now also understand the importance of knowing your desired outcome and reaching out to those for whom a match might be undiscovered. Thank you, Scott, your belief in me translated to important generational change. Those are everlasting. - **Shannon Leroux**, *CEO, Co-Founder SIVVA, Keynote speaker*

I have known Scott Manthorne for many years, both personally and professionally. He is a consummate professional, very well-connected, and highly skilled at bringing people together and facilitating introductions. If you have not met Scott, do yourself a favor and find an opportunity to connect with him and get on his radar. - **Stephen Wilson**, *IP, Sports and Entertainment Attorney at Beggs and Lane, RLLP*

Scott is one of the best networkers and connectors that I've ever met. He's leveraged his decades of meeting exceptional people to give us a chance to learn about great leadership from some amazing leaders. - **Tim Hayden**, *Co-Founder @ Xvisory and Stadia Ventures*

Scott is a master networker - who better to write the book! – **Tracy Deforge**, *CEO and Founder of The Players Impact*

FOREWORD

BY DAME DIDI WONG

I have always had a love of meeting people. Meeting strangers. Be it in the grocery store, in an airport lounge, in my children's school, at a live show, at a business event, at a friend's dinner party, or nowadays a lot on zoom or WhatsApp groups. In my opinion, people make the world go around. Every human being is unique and that is why it is such a fascinating topic when we talk about meeting people, as "networking." Sometimes that word comes with a negative connotation because it has an underlying tone of meeting people to get something from them. But in my world, it is a necessary word, a word that opens up doors, and a word that leads to what is most important in business: relationship capital.

I have only been focusing on building my network six years ago, after giving birth to my last two babies out of four. I decided to re-enter the world of entrepreneurship. And networking is absolutely necessary. I know I wrote that before, but I repeat it to emphasize how important it is.

I love networking. I get excited when I show up at a gathering of people I don't know, and I am not afraid to go alone. I don't need a companion as that may just distract me from meeting new people. Experiment it for yourself! I love the whole act of networking. From thinking about what to wear to the event and how I want to represent myself to the actual final act of networking, which is the exchange of information. Nowadays, as long as you exchange some kind of information, you have achieved your goal of networking: to be allowed to communicate with another human being in exchanging information regarding current projects, current asks or current capital raising. And since I do consider myself an expert in this field, I would look at it in a more advanced way by going one step further. Yes, once you have that new friend's number, email, Instagram handle, Facebook account name or WhatsApp number, you shouldn't stop there. You may want to ask the person you just got the information from, what is their favorite way of communication?

I personally don't mind giving out my phone number to people. I have a special way of making connections with others by taking a photo (so I remember them since I meet so many people all the time) and then I take their phone number so I can send them that photo. It has worked for me, and it gives a bit of a fun factor to the "networking." Once you ask, "What is your favorite way of communicating?" Or "Do you prefer texting or emailing?" Or "Shall I DM you?" then you know you have indirect permission to contact that person. And then from there, it is up to you to follow up or not.

It is important to note that networking is not just about making new friends and increasing your network. It is also about detecting if you do not want to keep in touch or delete people off your contacts. It's not about collecting people; it's about finding the gems of people with whom you want to surround yourself. And as many of my clients and audience from around the world know, after they hear me speak, I always say, "Your vibe attracts your tribe" So you do not have to be best friends with everyone. You want your network to be full of significant people. A dear friend once told me about keeping my LinkedIn contact list small as with LinkedIn, you can really just accept and request to be in contact with as many people as you want. It is a platform that has a high solicitation factor. And this friend is wise because he told me I would only want to look at the contacts that I have mutual friends with and to keep this group of contacts tight. And this is my friend Mr. Scott Manthorne.

Scott and I have been friends for almost five years which perhaps is not that much time, but if you knew the number of calls we have had in the five years, then you would see how this friendship has blossomed quite dramatically. Scott is the best at staying in touch. At first, he would email at least once a month to reach out to ask me for some time to do a call. In every new friendship, it is not strange for someone to reach out to book a call so that one gets to know one and see if there is synergy. But then Scott just continued reaching out, month after month and it became a pattern. A pattern that I recognize worked! He would reach out with no particular reason to speak but just to keep in touch. Of course, our calls end up being updates on each other's projects and what he can do to help me. He is, in my opinion, an "Ultimate Connector." It is always "What do you need right now? How can I help? Do you have anyone you need to meet?" And then I would tell him, "Yes, actually, I am working on a new TV show and need to meet some "sharks" who would be a good fit, or some ex-professional athletes, musicians, or anyone who would want to be an investor on a TV show, like a "Shark Tank." And he introduced me to Nelly, the rapper's manager or someone in the family office arena or someone who has a huge network of lightworkers. I also one time answered his question with, "Yes, I am working on a Martin Luther King Jr. project for my foundation and need to reach out to potential donors or anyone who really cares for MLK's movement and legacy." And he told me he knew someone for years and that this person actually marched with Martin Luther King, Jr.

Scott is that guy who knows someone who can connect you to anyone you really want to meet, not just domestically but internationally. More importantly, he is that guy whom others like and trust and would take the time to take a call if he introduced the parties to meet. He is that guy who connects people with unconditional love. With nothing expected in return.

Without having met Scott, I would not have met some of the biggest names in my life. I will not name too many names because there are so many. But without Scott, I would not have co-authored a book called "The Vine: Messages of Hope from Around the World" with the Dalai Lama, Dr. Jane Goodall, Andrew Jackson Young or Djimon Hounsou. I would not have met His Holiness Pope Francis and been working with him on his Foundation, I would not have met many Royalties of the world and received the Medal of Adwa from Prince Ermias of Ethiopia.

Scott opened the double doors to extensively grow my world and I cannot thank him enough.

I do have to note one important factor, and that is he would *not* introduce you if you are not the right fit. And that is what is so magical about Scott. He has an instinct for who will connect well with whom. He doesn't just blindly introduce people to each other, he has a methodical way of doing his "Inner Circles" or his "Roundtables." I am blessed to be one of the chosen ones as Scott likes to keep his circle tight.

If you have the fortune of picking up this book, I know Scott will sprinkle you with his magic through many of his interviews. The knowledge and experience from his large network will no doubt enhance your network and lead you to become a better networker.

INTRODUCTION

"If you don't treat your network like an asset, it won't perform like one."

I owe it all to the tech crash that occurred last fall ('22). Like many, I was immediately affected by this economic shift. Losing my job came without warning, and truly surprised me. As I sat in the Central Valley of Costa Rica (a favorite travel spot), it became evident that this life-changing event had a meaning. It's time to write my first book.

Over the years, there have been countless books written on the subject of networking. So many of them have proven to be quite valuable in my journey. I wrote this book to help convey real-world examples of networking. Many will read this book for business advice and my hope is that it will also help to highlight new ideas.

While the term is outdated, the results are the same. It's a skill set not taught in business school, and a topic many of us "hear about" by chance. It's complicated for many, uncomfortable for most, and something all of us need more work on.

Networking is part of our life. It drives our business success. It helps us build circles of friendships. It's the key to finding a job. It's useful when you want to know where to travel, what doctor to use, and how to get things done.

Fueled by over 25 years of experience in the industry, thousands of conversations, and hundreds of hosted events, this book contains stories from 80 executives in twenty countries. Relationships born from chance; others carefully curated with years of effort.

The authors: Eighty total, coming from twenty states and ten different countries. Our youngest is an 18-yr. old ParaOlympic competitor. Our most "seasoned" just turned 75 and has a rich history in Civil Rights.

The industries: The list is as diverse as the authors are. No matter what your profession, you will find a story to relate to.

The layout: Story format throughout. Plenty of quotes from the contributors. Lessons will be learned by the stories you connect with.

The outcome: I have three simple goals that I hope each reader achieves: 1). Give to Get. Expand your network by sharing it carefully with others.

2). Make more money, as the value of your network increases. 3). Save time with future networking activities, efforts and results

The wrap up: At the end of this book, I'll share my own story.

MY TOP TIPS

Unlike most books on this subject, I'm not going to write countless pages about how to network. It's been said many times before. Instead, I'll only share eight of my favorite tips to help improve your skills. Hope you like them!

Get Cracking! You met the person. Now FOLLOW UP and FOLLOW THROUGH. It's insane how many don't! If/when they do, it's been so long after the initial conversation the opportunity is no longer there.

Level Up: Slow down the networking. Too many of us are "over networked and under-connected." Quality is always better than quantity. Focus on upgrading your relationships.

Social Media Never Lies: People can see when you are online, who you have responded to publicly, what you have liked/ followed, and what you post. Be prudent. Be professional. Be appropriate.

Stop The Noise: Less follows, fewer likes, fewer connection requests, fewer posts. Streamline your efforts and reduce the barrage of communication and interaction. A little quiet does a person good.

The Three-Legged Stool: When you want to validate a person, an event, or a business opportunity, reach out to three people in your network for feedback.

Time Keeps Ticking Away: It's your most precious asset. Treat it right. Be smart with every decision about networking. The people you interact with. The events you attend. The way you manage your calendar. Every minute counts.

Two vs. One: Look in the mirror. One of the best secrets to networking is listening twice as much as you speak. Try it sometime.

What Did You Say? Yes, many call this an elevator speech. But it's even simpler than that. Pick a few keywords to share your point. You will be amazed by the response and the results.

AND MY PET PEEVES?

1. Being added to an email distribution list, without being asked.

2. Being asked for an introduction to anyone. REALLY?

3. Being late for a scheduled call or meeting, that you set up.

4. Receiving PDFs, presentation materials and other collateral BEFORE the first call.

5. Getting unsolicited LinkedIn, Instagram, Facebook requests to connect.

6. Hosting a call, or face-to-face only to have the other person go on a never ending rant about their product or service.

7. In a business conversation, never asking me what I want/ am looking for.

8. When someone name drops, brags about the relationship, but can't "back it up."

From the upcoming *Orchestrated Connecting* book written by David Homan, The Top Ten Terms for Connectors/Community Builders That Annoy Me

THE TOP TEN

The Collector - You've met this one for sure, knows a ton of people and keeps saying "I'll introduce you," but never does. They keep their cards close to the vest and don't share. They may truly care about you and be an awesome person, but they just don't ever deliver when they could help you so easily. I learned this from my friend Michael Roderick.

The Taker - Tries to use you to meet someone more prominent than you. Some people may refer to this person as a ladder climber, but I think it's worse. They may even say they know you better than they actually do to leverage their own relationships. Most importantly, they don't give back or reciprocate and can burn your bridges along with theirs.

The Honied Wasp - Knows lots of rich or influential people so thinks you will take a blind intro (without an opt-in) for someone who immediately pitches you on a project.

The (Mysterious) Lurer - Sometimes fishing lures are really colorful, but you still can't catch a fish if you suck at fishing. This individual reels you in with a mysterious need, and asks you for coffee or a call, and they know you just well enough to have you respectfully answer them, but then what they want of you could've so clearly been mentioned in advance, and now you're frustrated instead of maybe willing to help them – because you could've told them something in five minutes that now takes 30-60. You walk away and they don't even realize there was a pond full of fish you could've helped them with if they hadn't wasted your time by being vague.

The (Left and Right) Swiper - Someone doesn't check if you know someone (very easily) on LinkedIn or Facebook, or how you know them if you do, and then asks a favor of you while CC'ing that person. Now you're in the situation of blowing off the other person and looking unkind when you literally are just trying to clear your inbox and schedule some downtime within the next month - and clarifying what you can or won't do for this person.

The Selfish Assholes - The person/people who are so grateful to talk to you for 30 mins or an hour, and they just talk about themselves the whole time and don't ask anything about you. They walk away content, you walk away frustrated, someone knows nothing about your value.

The Valuator - Someone you meet whom, despite a strong introduction and context given, makes it clear they are busier and likely more important than you, so their response often implies an "are you good enough for me" attitude including asking to schedule a 20-minute introduction call, or make you come and meet them for 30 minutes near them.

The (Unfocused Nebulous) Nomad - This person really wants to shoot the shit but doesn't really get why you are meeting them or even the value of time. The meeting goes on and on as if they have more than an hour scheduled and you don't know what they do, how they live, or why you're spending the time meeting them. They do often have really good coffee.

The (Over Eager) Beaver - The person who keeps checking in because they just "happen to be wherever you'll be" all the time and doesn't get the hint you are too busy to hang out because your day is filled with purposeful meetings. They aren't bad, but they haven't helped you, and keep clinging.

The Subscriber - The person (likely from one of the above interactions) who somehow thought you wanted to be on a private BCC list (that you can't unsubscribe from without offending them) for what they write, and even worse also keeps following up asking you to do stuff they need because they somehow think meeting you (without listening to you) was enough to open all doors.

About David Homan: *David Homan is Vice President of Moonstruck Productions, co-founded by Paul and Kristina Dalio, whose work is at the intersection of feature film and impact. As the CEO of Orchestrated Connecting, David also runs a community of "connectors" and writes/speaks frequently about the power of connectivity. He is a classical composer and pianist, has an amazingly talented choreographer wife, and is a proud father of two artistic children.*

NETWORK INNOVATORS

India Lynn Wilkson has carefully crafted her network since college. Even when securing her first job in advertising she knew the importance of relationships, valuing them and keeping them close. "I make sure to maintain them. It's something that seems to be a bit lost even though it's really quite simple with a little bit of effort. When you know someone and trust them, great things happen." Combining her love for horses, entrepreneurship, and philanthropy, she has truly achieved success.

In one role, where she served as Marketing Director for the Atlanta Steeplechase, she sold over $3 million in corporate sponsorships, all by networking. "To me, networking needs to be a part of any successful business. I don't set aside time to network - I'm constantly finding opportunities to be engaged with people either in person or on social media. I help people connect and in return find amazing connections."

BEING A GOOD NEIGHBOR

"Helping others was instilled into me as a young child - I just can't sit by and watch others suffer. I was notified about a man who needed help but was rejected by many agencies because of his prison record. When I found out I turned to my fiancé and said, "We have to help!" I knew it was my purpose to step up and be a servant to this man who everyone rejected. We ended up hiring him to work in our warehouse. Slowly but surely, he crawled out of poverty, and after 10 years of commitment and lending a hand up, he is an active part of the community, has a great job with benefits, a beautiful apartment and most importantly is a part of our family. Networking on social media proved to be life-changing - people came together to raise money to put a deposit on the apartment, pay the first three-months rent and even furnished the entire apartment from a post on Facebook. The most important part of networking, which needs to be explained, is leaning into your current relationships, developing them, and working with them. Let your network help you because they genuinely want to."

HORSING AROUND

An avid equestrian and a marketing professional, India has been able to monetize her passion for networking. While sitting in a parking lot in Ocala, FL (the heart of horse country) after an unsuccessful trip to purchase a horse, India knew there had to be a better way. "My idea for an equestrian app to streamline the process of buying and selling horses was born through the frustration of not being able to find a sales horse or services without social media.

Launched in June '21, the app continues to grow through networking - it has over 300 horses listed and 250 equine services with the tagline, "Instantly Connecting Equestrians." The Mane Street Market app which caters to the Sport Horse community was built primarily though posting on social media and by word of mouth. This platform helps to compress the time curve in buying and selling horses as well as organize and manage relationships in the equestrian community.

TIME TO BE THE BOSS

In 2012 India started the journey of a successful side career with a well-known Network Marketing company. Instead of following the traditional model, India took a different approach and saw it as a way for equestrians to build a "side hustle" income that didn't depend on weather, clients, or sound horses. She dubbed it the "official skincare of the equestrian community" and it took off with 800 equestrians joining in the span of three years. Through intentional networking and growing the business, India replaced her corporate salary in two years, doubled it in four, and left her full-time job. Her personal team now totals 1,400 and has representatives in three countries.

"My network means so much more than business, people know they can always count on me to help if I'm able. Networking is a part of who I am - I pour into other networks as much as I can. My goal in order to connect on a personal basis is to pick up the phone - it disarms people because we've become a keyboard society. By picking up the phone people can hear the inflection in your voice and your passion for your purpose. They are much more likely to recommend you or your business after a personal conversation."

Scott MacGregor has been "making a difference his whole life." Author of the "*Standing O!*" book series, his life revolves around relationships. Everything in his business world points to delivering value, investing in others, and being unselfish. And from this many amazing initiatives, platforms and programs have been created. Some of them are below.

SOMETHING NEW

Started eight years ago, Scott wanted to create a company that could re-imagine the talent strategy business all while "giving back." Bootstrapping the business, he reached out to his gigantic and electric network to leverage his relationships. From these efforts, the idea of *Standing O!* came to life, as 100% of the proceeds are given to charity. This has led to four books in the series and is a testament to the people (5th book will come out this year).

The Standing O! series has over 200 authors represented, with well over 10 million social media followers. It has helped to drive numerous charitable endeavors, raise funds, and provide key visibility for many.

THE OUTLIER PROJECT

This amazing idea was born during Covid. In the late summer of 2020, Scott and his wife decided to take a road trip to Charleston, SC. On the way back, a discussion began about business and how they could reach a bigger audience. Realized the way to do so was to create a membership community.

In less than three months, The Outlier Project was up and running.

"People need to interact with accomplished and inspirational mentors who see the world through a different lens," says Scott. He assembled the first interactive conversation with several well-known entrepreneurs, athletes and bestselling authors, and the audience loved it! "We have done over 100 Legends Series live and interactive discussions and now have close to six hundred members in 33 countries and are growing rapidly."

In the fall of '23, Scott will host a four-day retreat with some true global influencers. It will bring together thirty select attendees who will receive a networking/ life experience unlike any other. And this is just the start!

THE TRUTH ABOUT NETWORKING

"I don't like the word because of the way people typically think of networking." Scott believes in building real relationships and being strategic. "The reason why I think I've been able to build a ton of real relationships, and others struggle, is because most people look for ways to monetize relationships. If they think they can't in a relatively short period of time, they simply don't invest in the relationship. Such a narrow focus keeps them from building a diverse business network."

His best advice? Be unselfish! Connect because you can, not because you should.

"You cannot make connections that are inequitable. Don't connect people when one of the people gets NO value. I only make introductions where there is shared value. I get requests all the time from people asking for introductions, but if they have no context or shared value, I don't make them. If I give an introduction to someone, I want both parties to be thrilled."

I have a thoughtful method that works for me, and I truly believe it can work for almost anyone. If yours doesn't come from a good place, it will never deliver the results you seek.

Stephen Meade is an American entrepreneur, executive and business founder who is passionate about creating companies that make a difference in the world. He has the ability to catapult an idea from pure concept to the creation of a thriving business. In the past 20 years, he has created, incubated and architected nine successful technology-based companies. He is a seasoned business advisor and leader who frequently speaks on the art of networking at executive leadership conferences and startup communities (i.e. executives, entrepreneurs, start-up founders, co-founders, students) around the world.

I'm In the middle of an impact event right now called COP28. The event will be hosted in Dubai and expects to draw over 50,000 executive attendees. Being a Network Innovator, Stephen decided to rent space, host an event, and make his presence felt. Utilizing a cinema, his format will include 12 different rooms, each featuring a unique topic. '

A true innovator in the industry, his real-world examples will help improve anyone's networking skills. Here are a few great examples:

HOW TO WORK A ROOM

Before I go to an event, I'll have a list of all the speakers put on a spreadsheet. Will have my VA go on LinkedIn to gain more information.

"I've learned within my process to ask a series of questions. It helps me better understand what they are trying to accomplish. It's a skill set that will help to elevate the conversation, save time, and give both clear answers."

When the speaker is done, they will walk off to the end of the stage standing in line like a robot for 30 minutes. I walk up and stand beside the speaker. Here are three great reasons why:

1. Listen to everyone pitching the speaker and learn what they are doing/who I want to talk to.

2. Listen to how the speaker answers.

3. When they are interested, someone else in the room handles things and I find out who they are).

Now I have the knowledge that everyone else never got. It's about efficiency. When returning from a big event, I take pictures of my business cards, send them to my Virtual Assistant, and have her enter them into my database.

KEYWORD NETWORKING

Utilizing his vast network and knowledge of databases, Steve relied on Google to help him identify key companies that will be participating. From this he was able to cross reference his LinkedIn connections, private database, and key relationships to begin to approach each as potential sponsors.

"The efficiency of hosting an event collapses the time curve of meeting people. Learn how to cut through the noise, when you are there, to meet the right ones."

THE NETWORK EFFECT

Since 1989, Stephen has been using ACT (database management tool) to record all of his business contacts. It now exceeds 30,000 executives and has detailed notes on each.

Over the years, he has presented at numerous universities. "I'm a legend at USC. I know how I met the people who introduced us, even what they were wearing. All have been labeled to industries, and this gives me an immediate record of our relationship."

TIME KEEPS TICKING AWAY

In 30 minutes, I can send out a customized email to up to 12,000 individuals. "I'm legendary for sending out my email. It's not sent out consistently but distributed organically when there is something to share (event, podcast, etc.). It's amazing the response I receive. Some of the most noted global executives will never respond...until they see something of commonality."

CHAPTER ONE

"Be the kind of connector people want to be with." - **Brandon Gutman**

A CAPITAL IDEA - DREW SHEINMAN

Early on, Drew knew he wanted to work in the sports industry. While in the University of Massachusetts Sports Management Program, he heard about a leadership management program at Major League Baseball. "I was doing a study on bringing a minor league to Worcester and worked my way to an executive in the league. He told me about the program."

An illustrious career creating/monetizing white space included being recruited to The Breeder's Cup World Championship. Said Drew, "Part of my role was to help horse racing become more mainstream."

Drew always wanted to be on the investment/capital side. "For years I met with people and did deals, but never found the right person/people to become partners with." Then while at Endeavor, Drew reached out cold to a company they wanted to align with. The private equity firm owner and he became friends, shared their passions, and realized a business partnership could be created leading to their successful investment firm.

"Part of what's behind this is that you need to be creative with whoever you want to be in front of. During the pandemic, my approach became more balanced. If I really like someone, I wouldn't hesitate to get on a plane and meet them."

Drew was an early adopter of LinkedIn, amassing nearly 22,000 contacts. "It's been an awesome tool to connect with people of relevance and value exchange." He continues to facilitate these relationships. A key strategy is to not overuse the platform, share select announcements and newsworthy items.

A FIELD OF VISION - AMOBI OKUGO

Even before his playing career began, Amobi knew it would be important to network for his slot on a team (as being traded often occurred in professional soccer). A 12-year career included international experience in both MLS and USL.

Moving from team to team, Amobi learned how to become part of a new community, a new team, and a new leadership role. "Being a center midfielder, my job was to connect offense to defense, players from side to side, and maintain a field of vision." This skill also helped identify other opportunities. Collaboration and partnerships have always been important. "Never know when you are going to use your network, but always have it."

His newest role is now as an entrepreneur. And with a successful playing career, it's been easy to get meetings. Even with an ease in networking, Amobi continues to do his research before a conversation. "I always try to find commonality, listening to what is shared and looking for ways to provide value. My model is to make five introductions, and ask for one back."

An early adopter of Social Media, he relies on Instagram, LinkedIn and Twitter amassing over 70,000 followers. Using 'bookmarks' on Instagram, Amobi helps connect brands to Influencers in health and wellness and sports fitness. A facilitator of sorts, he's quickly becoming known as one who can accelerate access to others.

With the playing days behind him, the focus now is on the business field. Managing relationships like he did a game; the next chapter is proving to be a big win!

A GLOBAL PERSPECTIVE - ISAAC RESHAD

Doing business between the Middle East and the United States has always been a balancing act. Since the pandemic, Isaac has carefully managed his exclusive circle of relationships with great care. "Things have changed since the pandemic. Business appetites, approach, political situation of the United States. It's not changing the network, or how we communicate. It's only changing the outcome."

Two things Isaac focuses on are authenticity and networking with discretion. Keenly aware of the value of time, he is careful to choose who he shares it with. "It's great to be friends, and I would rather become more personally connected with my key relationships instead of just adding new one after new one after new one"

With a very private client base, tactical networking has become a key to his long-term success. "One thing I've learned with networking is that I can't do the volume business. By keeping my network very tight (I like to keep it to 25 or less), I'm able to drive key opportunities forward. Conferences are great, but sometimes the audiences are too open. I tend to network peer-to-peer, and with executives who are servicing my target market."

A LABOR OF LOVE - DARRIN GRAY

It's been a life journey to be there for others. Always leading from the heart, Darrin has been purposeful in his quest to enhance the lives of all around him.

Darrin started networking professionally in 1990 when he took a job as a career placement director for a small school. "The nature of the job required me to reach out to business executives from multiple industries to help the students get great jobs in their chosen field of study."

Years later, Darrin was following his faith. It led him to a global ministry pastor called CUFI that was taking pastors pilgrimages to Israel. Not soon after, I was invited to bring some NFL players with us. In the first year a few were invited, along with a larger group. The next year the trip consisted of 20 NFL players, coaches and alumni. I sure enjoy influencing sports influencers, that in turn, influence others for the common good."

With the onslaught of social media, he's been careful to focus on what's important. Says Darrin, "I just started to get more serious on LinkedIn, Instagram, Facebook, Twitter, YouTube in support of my sports, media and missional projects. Reaching people across the globe with social media is important, and these platforms allow me to touch thousands of people each day instantly."

A LOVE FOR THE WATER - ERIC DAHLER, DHARDRA BLAKE

Meeting in Newport, Rhode Island in 2012, Dhardra and Eric were immediately drawn to each other while attending a private party. With both having a love for the water and yachting, soon their personal and professional lives were intertwined.

For both, strategic relationships have always been the key to success. After a brief period in the corporate world Eric began selling boats and yachts pursuing a career driven by his passion for the yachting lifestyle.

Eventually, the Hamptons became their summer base, and Palm Beach in the winter having put their own vintage yacht into the luxury day charter market. It's been a journey they have enjoyed the past 11 years. Dhardra added, "Through my day charter business, we had the natural network that followed the seasons, and found strong demand for yachting by the day."

Collaborating together, Dhardra and Eric discovered an appreciation for all types of boats and yachts. They are currently launching the Corinthian Yachting Club to provide membership-based access to a fleet of classic yachts and unique experiences as well as networking opportunities. "In the emerging shared economy tastes and engagement models in luxury and yachting continue to evolve," says Eric.

The ecosystem has been carefully built around the business. "Our mission is based around three pillars: bringing back classic yachting lifestyle that is simple and hassle-free; strategic networking through member events/cruises, and giving back / philanthropy."

Through their KINGFISHER Yachting venture they have donated cruises generating over $150,000 for local and global social impact. Eric and Dhardra continue to create distinctive, unforgettable experiences on the water, hosting athletes, celebrities, and CEOs of Fortune 100 companies.

"Since covid, we have seen the shift back to smaller groups, being outdoors and curated, boutique experiences, some incorporating emerging and iconic brands," explained Eric. "The relaxed vibe and camaraderie of a vintage yacht is very disarming and fruitful for networking and relationship cultivation." Said Dhardra, "Sometimes it's just about relaxing together. The beauty of it all is that relationships can be built, and we help to accelerate that."

A SECOND CHANCE - MAAYAN GORDON

For the rare few, life sometimes passes before our eyes. Her story is deeply personal, but the outcome is one that we all hope for.

With over 2.3 million followers on Tik Tok, Maayan Gordon is an influencer and has been providing strategic consulting the last three years. "My followers give me credibility and have led to lots of speaking opportunities." She has also leveraged the strength of the platform, understanding its growing strength in our culture.

More of a door opener and attention grabber, the Tik Tok platform provides great PR. "While a show will help you get exposure that day, Tik Tok can be used to open relationships with people who ignore messages on every other platform.

Comparing social media channels, this platform continues to outperform. "It's the best platform to feel deeply familiar as a person with a full-screen format. The culture of the platform is full of authenticity." Recently, Maayan posted that she had eggs for breakfast, easily relating to her followers.

"Tik Tok allows users to create their own personality, or Avatar. It gives others great insight as to how you experience life and provides close similarity to your personal life." Because of this, the business world is now paying attention.

A STAGE PERFORMANCE - ANDY ANDRUS

With a career spanning over 30 years, Andy played his guitar on too many stages to count. "I knew I wasn't going to be Jimmy Paige or Jimmy Hendrix, so I did something different." His unique style helped to land gig after gig, playing with many of the world's top bands. Playing differently was both a hindrance and a help. Says Andy, "Networking is not a pitch, it's how you play. You must talk to them, not at them."

Networking became vitally important as he often was in charge of finding the right venues to play, and the right audiences to connect too. "Putting a band together is no easy feat. You must match mindset, goals and harmonious compatibility. During my showbiz career, I performed in thousands of venues."

"When you go into business with someone, it's less personal and more academic. With musicians, it's quite subliminal. It's almost like finding a girlfriend and truly soulful. Almost like corralling cats and feels very fraternal."

Andy constantly lets his network know that a certain level of vetting is required, allowing him to minimize any unanticipated burden from a wasted introduction. "If you are doing an elevator pitch, be careful with it, and be authentic. It's always better to listen."

A VIRTUAL WORLD - CHRISTINA HELLER

Quickly, the world has transitioned to a virtual one. But for Christina it's been a way of life for many years. Sitting in the middle of virtual reality, she's been a constant force in steering the industry.

With a vision for the future, Christina founded and now hosts a social group based in virtual reality. "Back in 2019, we launched XR Social Club. It was inspired by the release of the Oculus Quest, and the excitement level was very high." Today the group meets weekly to socialize, network and play. It's truly a real-life experience.

31

The community acts like many. Friendships are built, and circles tend to be tight-knit. Gossip flows, different peer groups are formed, and relationships are built. "Most in our group are gamers, along with XR industry professionals. It's still not fully adopted by a more mainstream audience because we need greater headset adoption."

When Quest 2 came out, Christina noticed huge advances. With better hardware, better content, and better software, the adoption curve has increased. "VRChat is a social platform around for almost a decade. There are tens of thousands of worlds and really fun Avatars. It offers so many cool ways to play."

But like any networking platform, one must proceed with caution. "In VR, there are no rules. You have no idea who you are interacting with. It brings the best and worst out in the community." With XR Social Club, Christina enforces strict accountability measures, like a private club. This helps provide traditional benefits and civility.

"VRChat is my preferred platform. I'm always the hot dog, so people can recognize me." To her, it's as authentic as real-life interaction and offers a better experience than social media groups and chats." Over the years I have met many in VR chat, and from there went on to build meaningful friendships."

A WORLDLY VIEW - MARISSA FAYER

From Costa Rica to Switzerland, Marissa is always on the move. With a network exceeding 20,000 connections she has to rely on a complex system of email accounts, WhatsApp groups, LinkedIn conversations, and in-person events. Always seeking to connect at a diverse level, each opportunity is carefully evaluated.

"Everything is interconnected. It's no longer geographic for those of us who have a global footprint. When making new connections, I have a gut feeling and do my best to follow it. This helps me to stay away from relationships that I believe could be toxic."

Communication is now instantaneous. Text/IM and WhatsApp provide quick responses. But these mediums often create more work. "I receive pitch decks from many I know on WhatsApp, without my consent. Too many executives send things the way they want to, and never ask what my preference is. Because of this, I'll often delete their message without even looking at it."

ADAPTING TO CHANGE - CLAYTON AND EZRA FRECH

We first met on the stage at UCLA Anderson School of Business. At the ripe age of 10, Ezra Frech calmly took the microphone, sat on a stool, and welcomed hundreds of sports business executives to a daylong conference my company was hosting. And from that day forward, I have been in awe of the journey this adaptive athlete and his father Clayton have taken.

"When Ezra was born, we realized that the world needed more disability advocates. We were environmental advocates at the time, but quickly realized the environment had plenty of advocates, and the disabled community did not." After years of engaging in the disability community to learn and understand what resources were available for Ezra, and what were not, they stumbled upon their higher purpose.

When Ezra was 8 years-old, Clayton took him to his first Paralympic competition, the Endeavor Games in Oklahoma, and he immediately knew his path. "It was like a lightning bolt moment for me. I realized that the opportunity to compete in Paralympic sports needed to be more accessible, especially in Southern California which has over 20 million people! I thought to myself, this is one of those things that I am meant to do on this planet. Let's go figure it out."

Two years later the Angel City Games was launched. Clayton and his family drew from their strong network of relationships for help. "Many people were interested in helping us in those early stages, but we didn't know what we didn't know." The organization, in 2016, pivoted to Angel City Sports and has been growing ever since, adding sport training and loaner equipment to their programs.

Fast forward to 2022, and Angel City Games hosted 144 training sessions across 21 different adaptive and Paralympic sports.

Clayton, Ezra, and their family use sport to advocate for people with disabilities. "I know how challenging it is to live with a disability. Everywhere we go in public, there are people staring and pointing fingers and whispering. Angel City Sports is really providing a family, a community, a space for people to feel like they fit in. It's more powerful than any medal I'll ever win," said Ezra.

Looking to strengthen and grow the Angel City community, they rely heavily on social media. "As the world adapts, so do we. We see social media as the most cost-effective way to reach potential athletes going forward. And we feel there is tremendous opportunity for us to tell our story, and the stories of our athletes, in the digital and social media space."

While Angel City has grown tremendously in the ten years since inception, Ezra's journey has been pretty remarkable as well. He earned a spot on the US Paralympic Track and Field team in 2019, as a 14-year-old. That year he won gold at the Junior World Championships, two silvers at the Pan American Games, and was in the finals for all three of his events at the World Championships. And then, in 2021, he competed in the postponed Tokyo 2020 Paralympic Games, coming in 5th in the high jump and 8th in long jump. He was only an inch from the podium in the high jump.

As the lead ambassador for Angel City, Ezra continues to drive awareness for adaptive and Paralympic sports. In fact, he has grown his social media following substantially since the Tokyo Games, and now sits at over 400,000 followers on Instagram and TikTok. Ezra hopes to prove to all children with disabilities that nothing is impossible. "Go after that dream, give it everything you have and make it happen because, at the end of the day, we truly have the fate of our potential in our hands."

QUOTES

"Always remember to pace yourself." - *Samantha Katz*

"Don't prejudge someone by their title, their company, their industry, or the power of their network. Some of the most profitable transactions you complete will come from a channel that was never even known about." - *Jason Ford*

"Having relationship capital allows you to use the network in ways you may not have imagined- when I joined my present company as COO, we were able to double the revenue of the organization in 12 months relying heavily on my relationship base and mentoring others on how to capitalize on theirs." - *Greg Santore*

"Hyper focus on what you want to network into. I'm going to be stricter with my travel, even if it's into the city. I often encourage meetings to happen where I live, and not the other way around. Time is money. The cost is now double (not just the actual expense, but also the time invested in traveling to/from)." - *Alice McLaughlin*

"I have succeeded in life because of networking. While most people want business to come to them, I've gone out of my way to build relationships....especially for business." - *Luciane Serifovic*

"If you don't have the conversation, you will never have the result." - *TJ Rives*

"It's hard keeping up with everyone all the time. We are all SOOO busy … If you don't have set calendar days, scheduled calls, or other ways to bring the relationships together, you may miss out on opportunities." - *Elisabeth Flach*

"It's not the business you close, it's the conversation you open." - *Ken Hubbard*

"Know what's behind the numbers. It helps both sides to understand the tendencies of the user/company. Keep notes in file for each, as it will always be there as a reference." - ***Craig Handley***

"Life is a collection of experiences and relationships. Used correctly we can elevate our business to all kinds of impactful levels." - ***David Shtief***

"Never turn down the opportunity to have a conversation." - ***Carrie Nikitin***

"Oftentimes work comes full circle when another competitor doesn't deliver." - ***Kenny Hazlett***

"One-on-one conversations with a genuine connection have always made it easier for me to move forward." - ***Alycia Powell***

"With select executives, my trust in them helps me to make the decisions that they make. With those I don't know, my process needs to slow down and be much more cautious in moving forward on a business transaction. The majority of my time is spent with those that I know, or that my trusted network knows." - ***Isaac Reshad***

"You have to have some private time. But the real business relationships have to be more than transactional. The better it is, the deeper you go. You have to have each other's back." - ***Russ Rieger***

"Your name will always be mentioned in rooms you will never be in." - ***LaVonne Idlette***

CHAPTER TWO

"Too much activity breeds too little response." - ***Christina Heller***

ALWAYS ON THE GUARD - NEIL HOBDAY

Entering the army at 21, Neil joined the Scots Guards and spent five years serving. He became one of the youngest captains ever and enjoyed a rich experience.

Soon he entered the business world, securing a prestigious job. Immediately, Neil understood the importance of relationships. Trained to report to a hierarchy, he didn't realize even the youngest secretary would be evaluating him. "I learned straight away that if you don't hold your weight, you won't hold a job." It caused a radical shift in his attitude.

Neil quickly re-engineered and reinvented himself. Soon, he began to see significant results in his business goals. His career took him through many prestigious jobs, including a long stint with IMG.

His most recent post was as the Chief Executive at Guards Polo Club. Neil attributes securing this job from maintaining his relationships in the military and continuing to expand an impressive network. "I always felt at ease managing royalty, heads of state, actors, musicians and industry titans. The trick was knowing how to communicate to this audience, listen more, talk less, under promise and over deliver," said Neil.

"In the way I work, I keep my relationships warm. It's a very rifle-shot approach. If I'm meeting or in the company of well-known, wealthy, and successful people, I've always managed to engage on a personal level." Neil goes on, "Never ask for anything. It's often unexpected and truly refreshing."

Neil always is careful to discuss something each will be interested in. "Preparation is very important." To this day he continues to maintain the role as an advisor to key politicians within the government.

With a global resume, and relationships to match, Neil has learned many valuable lessons worth sharing:

- Everyone is as nervous and lacking in confidence as you are. Everyone feels the same.
- If someone promotes being a certain way, the opposite is probably true.
- Time spent in reconnaissance is seldom wasted.
- When you do get unique individuals to talk, and really listen, you will learn so much more.

AN AMAZING RACE -- LAVONNE IDLETTE

Even in college, Lavonne knew how important relationships were. "As a student-athlete, it was important to build strong connections with my professors. With my competition schedule, I often missed classes and tests, and needed to make them up."

From a storied career on the track, she was soon competing to enter the Olympic Games (competing in 2012 for the Dominican Republic, 100-meter hurdles). "There was definitely an 'in crowd' that helped athletes get into races, and I wasn't." Soon, Lavonne changed her representation. Immediately, her calendar was booked with races on a regular basis.

"My business actually started at the Olympics," says Lavonne. When competitors realized she was also an attorney, many started asking for her help with representation. This soon led to her practice growing all over the world.

A chance call from the producers at Survivor led to an invitation to participate in Season 32 of The Amazing Race. "Initially I was contacted for one show and turned it down.

But I liked the concept of the other, shared my story and was invited to participate."

Nowadays, her schedule is more rigid as she utilizes a booking system for meetings, for personal affairs, and for fun. "I seek to speak with those who have the greatest impact," says Lavonne. And with social media, she can easily communicate with and follow her target market.

As a mother to a newborn child, Lavonne still attends events and key masterminds. "There is a community of men and women who have their children all the time. This is one of my tribes." A champion of balancing work and personal life, she is often asked to speak at retreats. "Being authentic helps me to connect closer to others."

AN OPEN DOOR POLICY - BRITTANY DUNN AND KRISTI WELLS

As military spouses, Brittany and Kristi have traveled the country. With each new base and increase in rank, their relationships flourished. But this also leads to tighter circles, making it a challenge for many to gain access. So, they decided to take an inverse approach, always saying yes to a conversation and talking to anyone who had interest.

"We all have to be networked together. Of course, there is a vetting process, but I'm often surprised what may come from it. You should be willing to follow the rabbit trail, and not be too critical on the outcome." This has led to an open-door policy with a layered approach. Weighted by the strength of the relationship, their calendar remains flexible for the unknown.

"On LinkedIn, we have a tool we use that sends customized messages directly from our accounts and approaches contacts based on what we are doing. It could be seeking event attendees or donor drives. One convo led to a healthcare executive, and introduction to another, and then a national partnership. We feel over 200 positive outcomes have been created."

"We don't know what we don't know. Coming from a humble spirit it's important to be lifelong learners."

AUTHENTICITY ALWAYS PAYS OFF - ALYCIA POWELL

Like most of us, Alycia didn't get into the idea of networking till attending Law School. Jumping right in, she attended her first event with others in sports and entertainment, dressing in a way she felt the audience would appreciate. "I had an advisor that sat me down and explained to me that I wouldn't be taken seriously if I didn't dress very conservatively. He was wrong."

Entering the workforce, Alycia knew she would be challenged when networking. "Because I was just out of law school, I decided to lead my conversations off with this." It paid off, and she began to build her network immediately. "Always be yourself. Don't hide your personality, what you like, or who you are."

Now traveling the globe for a variety of business projects, Alycia is quick to seek out areas of commonality when starting conversations. "Authenticity always pays off. I'll never forget that."

BE KEEN TO LISTEN - IAN O'DONNELL

A natural for sales and marketing, Ian's path started elsewhere. "I was a finance guy, trading and doing bookkeeping. Soon, I realized it wasn't for me," said Ian. He quickly understood one of his gifts was relationships and building them (for myself and others).

Like many, his career has been diverse and unique. Ian traveled the globe, and in one job role was tasked with convincing general managers to buy into their company program. Not soon after, in conversation with a mentor, he told Ian to "pursue what makes you passionate. He knew he wanted to get involved with sports somehow.

Finally, that day came. "Our company had a huge NASCAR program, and I want to be involved. So, I started by volunteering." Ian had no experience but saw the opportunity. So, he started taking lead roles. "One day a manager asked me to come interview with me for a promotion. It was the break I was looking for."

"Business is all about being there. Listen to what they say. Do whatever it takes. Be present," said Ian. He knows the importance of building relationships that are business relationships, and those become friendships. Working closely with an industry business association called Brand Innovators, he continues to look for ways to improve. "Ultimately I'm here to connect people and make things easier."

"My talents have helped me to uncover additional business opportunities outside of my key job role. Companies are really looking for entrepreneurs to work for them within the company. They want the best creators, knowing even more business will come back," said Ian.

BEST OF THE BAY - BRIDGETTE BELLO

In Tampa Bay, FL, Bridgette Bello is truly the center of the business universe. Her network is second to none and comes from years of careful curation and endless efforts to build relationships. "Running my own community allows me to continue to choose the company I keep, more so now than ever."

Almost five years ago she decided to leave the corporate world and launched Tampa Bay Business and Wealth (TBBW). Running the premier magazine in the market, her reach is impressive. "We have about 15,000 who get our monthly print magazine and another 10,000 get our newsletter email twice a week. 20,000 engage monthly, with our website and 50,000+ are exposed to our social media channels on a consistent basis."

Introductions and referrals now come at an amazing pace, with many of them through the executives featured in each month's cover stories. "Events are carefully built with a curated audience of 150 executives, allowing a peer-to-peer networking opportunity. Many local CEOs didn't know each other and met because they were on our cover or attended a TBBW event."

In recent years, engaging with local non-profits has become even more important. It's allowed for additional relationship building and brand trust for both the non-profit and TBBW. And it's a great way to support the community. "We make the connections of relevance happen, because we can," says Bridgette.

BOWL ME OVER - ELISABETH FLACH

At last year's Las Vegas Bowl, Elisabeth was reorganizing her day while sitting in the media room. A random conversation started with several of the interns, discussing how they could network at an upcoming event. What happened next could happen to anyone.

Elisabeth Flach is a master of conversation, knowing when to talk, when to ask questions, and when to listen. Things quickly turned to basketball, where her son is actively seeking a college scholarship. Also in the circle was a highly accomplished executive with a rich history in the professional game. Fast forward, and it turns out they both also lived in the same town. Small world!

"Too many people network for business, too few networks for relationships. At some point, many will be leveraged for profit. Most don't understand this point. It's too transactional," says Elisabeth.

Leaning on Linked for business, she utilizes it to expand her global network and close select deals. Careful to construct an appealing profile, her connections quickly eclipsed 5,000 executives. "I've always found that networking for me is one of two things: Showing up with no idea who will be there, I always seem to meet the right person at the right time. It never fails. Or I go to an event, knowing there is a guest list/RSVP form. I'll check out the attendees in advance and do my best to find the individuals I want to meet."

CAN YOU HEAR ME NOW? - NICOLE MIDDENDORF

Constantly evolving, Nicole is on a quest to have her voice heard. "I've learned a lot over the years. It's completely changing how I'm doing things."

Utilizing technology to communicate her message and bring people together, Nicole has become a master of media. Knowing LinkedIn is for business she launched her own set of websites and special projects. "More than ever our networks are thriving, and connections are still valuable."

Leaning on her Facebook community, she's been able to organize unique travel experiences. Taking a trip for 20 people to Napa, everything started from simple conversations online. "Sharing is caring," says Nicole. "Be the best you can be and be happy."

And now she will push even harder, with a goal of expanding her social media footprint 10x. To reach the next generation, video content will be added. And soon, she will add a podcast and expand her footprint to additional social media channels. Can you hear her now?

CREATING MAGIC - ROB AND KERI STUART

In the business world, the success of a company is often directly related to the connections that its owners have with their network. This is especially true for Rob and Kerri Stuart, the owners of a successful full-service travel agency, Creating Magic Vacations, an Authorized Disney Vacation Planner.

Rob and Kerri have always had a passion for travel and a love for Disney. In fact, they initially became travel agents back in 2008 part-time and later purchased a travel franchise because they wanted to travel more and help other people do the same. They initially sold cruises and the more they traveled throughout the world, one thing they noticed was whenever they were at Disney, their live videos and social posts would get the most response. So why not do more of that to expand their social media reach? This also was the start of networking with people they had never met in person.

They started their podcast, "Disney Travel Secrets," in March of 2017 and it quickly grew in popularity. This led them to leave the franchise and start their own travel agency in 2018. And then a big move from St. Petersburg to Orlando in 2022, just to be closer to Disney.

In less than five years, their team of Travel Agents with Creating Magic Vacations has grown nationwide, all working from home. And all of that is a result of taking a network of podcast listeners and having offline conversations - whether it is to become a travel agent with their agency or book their next vacation.

What makes their business unique is the fact that the vast majority of their agents have no experience in the travel industry. Rob and Kerri do this on purpose. They look for people who have a passion for Disney and are looking for a way to start a part-time business, while doing something that they are passionate about. Rob and Kerri love "Creating Magic," and they do just that by training their agents on a regular basis. Not just about travel, but how to run and grow a successful business and the importance of your network. Each January they host their annual conference called Agent Palooza at Disney. That's how important in-person meetings are to them.

They strongly believe that technology will never replace a real, in-person connection. Technology can help with systems but doesn't replace building a relationship. This is why they prioritize face-to-face meetings and encourage their agents to get involved in their local communities.

They find that the best and most loyal clients are a result of taking time to get to know the individual style of travel and that no one trip fits everyone. They teach their Agents to do the same. Get on the phone and don't hide behind email or text.

Their advice for anyone looking to build a network is to get comfortable getting in front of people. Ask a lot of questions, take the time to get to know them and really listen.

While it's easy to get caught up with fancy online tools, social media and websites, Rob and Kerri attribute much of their success to constantly creating a connection online whether it be from a social media post, an email newsletter or a podcast and then taking those relationships offline. This is as easy as a simple phone call or a meeting over coffee. And this is at the heart of Creating Magic for their agents and their clients.

CREDIBILITY COMPRESSES THE TIME CURVE. - GREG ANTONIOLI

Building inspectors are dying and retiring. So now I have to start the process all over again. Our reputation is strong, so it's only a matter of asking the new executive for a quick introductory meeting and "jump-start" the relationship. Another example is the outgoing manager helping to pass the baton to his replacement, which oftentimes leads to a highly functional connection with credibility.

QUOTES

"Always establish the same dictionary with the person you are talking to." - *Stephynie Malik*

"Be interested, not interesting, listen intently, and ask your conversation partners questions about them!" - *Mark Moyer*

"Be patient with people, because when you feel like you are operating at a high level. The expectation may not meet the outcome. Part of building relationships is humanizing those that you are sitting across the table from. Give them the same benefit you would want with your process." - *Alan Pavlosky*

"Connecting people to their goals and dreams is my purpose and I'm lucky enough to have found my purpose in life. Many people don't find it for themselves. It's truly a blessing." - *Jeff Tutor*

"Don't be afraid to ask for what you need. You will get there, just dig." - *Carrie Nikitin*

"Don't try to be everything to everybody." - *Dave Sanderson*

"I follow the simple axiom that 'people support what they help to create.' Rather than asking someone to help me, I listen first to what they care about and to see how we can connect, collaborate and co-create. I start at the heart level, which often leads to the business level, and then ultimately to the spiritual level." -*Darrin Gray*

"If you really want to connect with people, you need to have real conversations." - *Rob and Keri*

"It doesn't matter how you said it, it matters how someone heard it." - *Maayan Gordon*

"Last April at a Women's Conference in Switzerland, I was following a certain fund, and identified the person I wanted to speak with. So I waited until a networking break, where things were more social, and approached her and said: "How can I help you." I'm now the U.S. partner for the company." - **Marissa Fayer**

"Learn how to ask questions that enable you to find what you and another person have in common which is unique - tell me you also attended HBS . . . OK, that's nice . . . but tell me that you were born in a small town in Kansas, attended public school and also love the KC Chiefs, Royals and Jayhawks, now let's go get some BBQ and see how I can help you." - **Todd E. Benson**

"Never be afraid to ask for help........you never know who someone knows or what they are willing to do unless you put the question out there." - **Tiffany Smith**

"People may forget what you say, but they will always remember how you make them feel." - **Jason Ford**

"So much of our lives are transactional, where people seek to get something out of an exchange. At NEXUS we invest in building bonds that last a lifetime, where someone always has your back." - **Rachel Gerrol**

"Three things to say. Who I am. What I care about. What do you care about?" - **Rob Vaka**

"We can make great strides as founders by not focusing on *how*, but rather on who. It's the *who* that help your business grow. *How* will only frustrate you." (Dan Sullivan). - **David Shteif**

"Without key knowledge on a potential networking partner, the only way to validate their contacts is to just have conversations and learn how you can benefit one another." - **Hayden Kopser**

CHAPTER THREE

"Ask meaningful and sincere questions, listen intently to responses, and seek to add-value and focus on the merit of the conversation as opposed to an outcome. Try this and see what will happen." - *Danny Hughes*

DON'T LET GO OF THE STRING - MARY KUREK

A veteran in the business development space, Mary, who is the founder and CEO of Frontrunners Development, Inc. has always made North Carolina her home. In this interview, she shares a bit about her story and some advice she'd give other CEOs.

"My company has been evolving for about 16 years. Some of those years include business consulting, the authoring of a business networking book, professional introductions for the games industry, and publishing the first global online business networking magazine. About eight years ago, we evolved into a global business development agency focusing on the world's problem solvers and working at connecting impact partners. The migration to today's agency with a global community of what we call 'Frontrunners' happened pretty fast, actually. I was at an extraordinary conference in the Research Triangle Park area where I had that amazing opportunity to meet in person three people from my Frontrunners community. Sitting down in the hotel room after the first day I started to realize that I needed to start curating these connections I had been developing through the interviews I had conducted for my online magazine. I texted an advisory board member, and he told me, "You need to build an organization called Frontrunners League of Social Impact Innovation. And he started laying out the foundation that has brought me to where I am now."

The Frontrunners League is a global organization spanning 76 countries with 550 executives, innovators, and diplomats who have been interviewed for the Frontrunners Innovate Media Platform, owned and produced by Frontrunners Development, Inc.

With such an expansive network, Mary continues to rely on a few tools to manage her relationships. "A calendar system has saved my life, as it's impossible to coordinate calls across such a diverse global network for nonstop meetings that often require some follow-up immediately afterward. I also utilize a virtual assistant for additional support."

As for advice regarding creating important connections, Mary shares this: "If you look at an introduction as just a friendly courtesy, that's how those who are introduced will look at it. Don't let go of the string once you have it. It becomes your responsibility to follow through." Mary understands this value. "I once let go of the string when I had made introductions that I really didn't think would go anywhere. The parties I introduced created a partnership and ended up winning an award for their project. That actually happened twice with the same client. Lesson learned. I had the string; it was on me to keep it."

FINDERS, MINDERS, GRINDERS, AND BINDERS - STEPHEN WILSON

In connection with his global intellectual property (IP), sports, and entertainment law practice, Steve has enjoyed building a substantial business from networking. The mixture of attending events, participating in online platforms, and colleague introductions fuels a healthy pipeline of new relationships.

No matter where or when it seems that networking is always evident in his business career. "A significant part of my business comes from networking and referrals from clients. It never stops. The more proactive I am, the more opportunities present themselves."

Whether attending international trade events or connecting with clients and contacts during Super Bowl Week, Steve will be there. "I enjoy connecting with many clients and friends at these events, and often leave with exciting new projects."

A simple philosophy, but not all adhere to it. It is sometimes said that there are finders, minders, grinders, and binders.

Finders are rainmakers with a knack for spotting opportunities, facilitating introductions, and generating new business.

Minders are managers who are skilled at managing ventures, projects, and personnel and maintaining long-term relationships.

Grinders are workhorses who are not afraid to roll up their sleeves and devote the time and energy necessary for a project to succeed.

Binders are networkers and connectors who enjoy bringing people together, facilitating introductions, and building and maintaining relationships. Some may naturally gravitate toward one of these roles or another based on their personality, interests, and skills, but they should not be afraid to step out of their comfort zone and cultivate skills in other roles that could open new doors.

His simple advice is to sow the seeds. Some seeds may immediately sprout, while others take time to grow. "Recently, a decades-old introduction and relationship led to new opportunities and strengthened the friendship at the same time."

FOLLOW THE YELLOW BRICK ROAD - STACY GRANT

Always a dreamer, Stacy has been relentless in her pursuit to find the right pathway. As a single mom in Michigan, her networking journey started while being a massage therapist. "When I moved to an affluent community in Michigan, I realized that networking at the high-income level brought the most opportunity."

Her journey crossed many more business sectors, and states, as Stacy eventually landed in Florida. Along the way, she relentlessly pursued learning opportunities and attended self-development conferences to learn how to become a better entrepreneur.

A casual conversation with a friend soon changed her world. "Why don't you sell boats?" Good question, as Stacy loved industry, the water and the lifestyle. "I decided to visit local offices and learn more about it." But with no job and no experience, many passed on her hiring request. But this was just an obstacle, and not an end.

Finding the yachting company, she wanted to work for, Stacy got to work. Reaching out to the founder and being as authentic as she could made the difference. He loved her, felt she would be great at the job and made the hire. Through her network, telling everyone what she was doing, and posting often on social media, Stacy ended up selling eleven boats that year, and broke all kinds of records...with no experience.

"I still have boats I work with from social media. You can meet anyone you want on Facebook, LinkedIn, wherever." As I moved through different industries, my audience changed, and I had to adjust those I was wanting to influence. To grow your reach, Stacy suggests you change your audience to those who will buy what you sell. Even now, it's not uncommon for her to be approached at boat shows by someone she's never met. "I know you," many say. Visibility for her is the key to success.

Want to follow *your* Yellow Brick Road? Here are some of her tips:

1. Always elevate your network (hers exceeds 50,000 on social media).

2. Be a "solution seeker," find ways to work around things.

3. Don't be everything to everyone.

4. Figure out what your brand is on social media and stick to it.

5. Pick the three things that you want to be (family, travel, business).

6. Show people who you are. Authenticity means everything.

GROWING PAINS - GIBSON HARNETT

Recently moving to New York City, Gibson has developed many new relationships and contacts through in-person conversations instead of relying solely on technology. "Mutual respect has been tarnished as it is easier to see someone as an avatar or name in a phone, rather than having a substantive interaction. Turn off the tech and have coffee with someone. Get out of your comfort zone. Try something new. Challenge yourself."

"The word networking is traditionally associated with business-related activities, but in reality, every conversation you have is about making connections. It's hard to know when and where that important connection may happen so never burn a bridge, never hold a grudge, and treat everyone with respect. This is my brand."

As he came into the workforce, Gibson saw LinkedIn as a way to connect, keep up to date on business news, and follow key individuals. Knowing you are the company you keep, he's been focused on connecting to those that line up with his current business goals. Despite recognizing the value of social media platforms, Gibson has realized there is much more to networking.

"I think there is a multi-tiered approach to maintaining and building relationships. There are the social media personas, Instagram likes, and twitter retweets. While these people can be important for branding and developing an audience, they are often superficial connections.

The next level of relationships are people that we have crossed paths with at some point, but for one reason or another we no longer maintain direct contact. These may be Facebook friends, old high school teammates, or former colleagues.

The final group of people are the meaningful relationships that we actively maintain and nurture. This is your inner circle."

One thing that Gibson emphasized was the importance of elevating people from the middle tier to his inner circle.

"The sole reason for this is to humanize each relationship, whether business or personal. The importance is nuanced - the 'networking' will take care of itself."

HOLD ON TO THAT CARD! - JASON FORD

Starting out in the banking and hospitality space, Jason soon found himself leading a career in public service focused primarily on economic development. An early adopter of LinkedIn, he has become a legendary collector of business cards.

His fascination started in the early 1980s. "I remember going to restaurants and collecting cards off the boards there. My parents helped me collect cards, too." But as life got busy, and Jason's professional journey took many turns, he soon forgot about the collection.

"One day my mom showed up with over 1,000 cards. It re-ignited my interest, and I now made a point to go back and reconnect with past executive connections from time to time."

On a tactical level when a team member says, "We are going to New Jersey to meet an executive," I go through the cards — sometimes for inspiration of others to meet in the same market — and other times to cross reference past conversations that need to happen again. To Jason, they mean more to him than just a name and a number. "Long before I knew what a Rolodex was, I cataloged each card, making notes to remind me of the value of each conversation."

Sometimes it's like a walk down memory lane. "I often show people the cards, my network, my relationships. It's the multiplier effect of who you know, who they know and so on."

Fast forward to today. Everyone wants to scan the QR code, and he's still writing notes on the back of cards (now has more than 8,000). "This allows me to be selective in who I want to activate from my collection. It's within an arm's length of my office."

Recalling one of Jason's favorite stories, "I was at a global sports conference this week and asked for permission to write on their card. It creates an amazing touch point to reflect on the original conversation. It also helps to deepen connections in a faster way and shows how much I value the relationship."

INTENTIONAL INTERACTION - DARRAH BRUSTEIN

A recognized global thought leader, Darrah is an expert in helping others create a life of meaning. Her teachings are simple (and rooted in the age-old wisdom of Dale Carnegie): It all stems from Know, Like and Trust. Below are some true words of wisdom she shares that stem from this philosophy: "When looking to connect with someone with whom you've not spoken in quite some time and have an ask for them: call out the potential awkwardness. Pay them a sincere compliment, letting them know why you're reaching out and value them for this reason specifically. Do your best to veer the relationships to just that (a relationship), rather than a transaction."

"Every action is underpinned with an intention. Two seemingly identical actions might be entirely different based on the intention. A tool (like social media, for example) is natural until an intention is paired with its use."

"There's a lot of talk about offering value in relationships. I agree with this so long as it's not used as a tool to manipulate to ultimately see how you get to what you want more quickly. A common concern people share when thinking about this concept is, "What do I have to offer?" Everyone has value to offer, you included. A great example of this is something you see at a lot of Fortune 100 companies called reverse mentorship where a newer member of the company mentors a much more senior and seasoned one. Reframe the way you look at how you can help others. When someone asks you for your support or accepts the offer of it, that's a gift to both of you."

"Keep in mind that every relationship takes time to build and nurture. While some things may speed that up like shared history, a trusted mutual introduction, or the quick development of rapport, there is no true shortcut to this. Take your time."

"Don't write off or judge people when you meet them because you think they can't 'do anything for you'. This is short-sighted.

I prefer to make my 'metric of evaluation' whether or not I enjoy their company. So, what if they don't seem like they can help me. We have a limited number of people with whom we can be in a relationship (155, give or take, if you believe Dr. Dunbar's research) so I prefer to fill those 'slots' with people whose company I enjoy. Keep in mind, as well, that everyone is a representative of their Rolodex and knows many other people to know they could connect you... once there is trust."

"Over the course of your life, you will see that there's a spectrum you'll traverse of times when you're hunting versus gathering for new relationships. Let's say you've entered a new industry. You may be more on the proactive, hunting, side of the spectrum. As time passes and you grow your relationships as well as a stellar reputation, you'll be able to gather more and sift through introductions and opportunities that come your way more passively. This phase offers more leverage and is more sustainable over time. Keep in mind that you will not become immune from meeting new people. Use those opportunities to stay curious and open."

"It's common to want to get to the stage where you are well known, have credibility, and a reputation that speaks for you. However, just like the idea of 'overnight successes' is mythical, so is this. Put in the time and find ways to build a solid network that you enjoy so you want to keep doing it."

"Don't feel like you have enough time to invest in the building and nurturing of relationships? Consider this: Dedicate 5-10 minutes a day to reach out to three people. Look at their Instagram stories and respond, comment on social media platforms, send a voice text, call for a 5-minute catch-up conversation. When you extrapolate that out, that's three people per day, five days a week. That equals 15 touch points with your network per week, or 60 per month by spending 5-10 minutes a day. Put it into your workflow however it works. Bucket a slot of time each day or a bigger bucket once a week. It won't work if it doesn't work for you."

INSURING A GOOD OUTCOME - HAYDEN KOPSER

A lifelong student of mastering relationships, Hayden knows it all comes down to the basics. "People like to have their name pronounced correctly, be treated well, feel valued, and know your gestures come from a good place."

Often attending key events, he is keen to know who is going to be there. "Determine if it's focused enough. Consider the ratio of useful contacts you could meet. Some networking has no value beyond keeping your skills sharp, and some groups are too disorganized to benefit from joining. Joining them becomes a time commitment, and our time is our most valuable asset. Be careful not to overload your calendar with events thinking that it will produce results. Being busy does not automatically equal being successful, in fact it can be a distraction."

Hayden has a process to his conversations and follows the same plan every time. "Ask how you can provide knowledge, information and advice to others with the assumption that karma will come back in the future." He also is careful to show where value can be added, while supplying complementary recommendations. "I have yet to meet someone who has knowledge and contacts but doesn't in turn help others to get connected. If you want to be selfish and successful, your goal should be to help others."

Try to leave a conversation with an intentional action point like setting a follow-up call, or a time to meet in person at a specific date. Per Hayden, "Good networkers will always maintain detailed notes and utilize them to move the relationship forward. Ask lots of thoughtful questions and listen well to what your contacts say until they are done speaking. The answers you receive will guide the direction of the conversation and answer questions and supply useful information you did not think to ask for."

IT PAYS TO LISTEN - DANIEL HUGHES

In spite of his severe hearing loss, Danny is an exceptional listener. He learned from early childhood to read lips and pay attention to the smallest of details. His philosophy is simple:

Listening is an intentional exercise. To architect a world class network, get to know people, what drives them, and learn how you can be supportive in their future goals. (Career advice, business strategy, personal ambitions.) "The power to support other people's relationship development efforts is the most impactful networking activity."

One of his examples is about a gentleman named Richard, who was the business partner of a known sports personality. "I learned about his work in Africa, partnerships that would be of value, and what their future goals were. From this conversation, I was able to find the right fit which led to a truly meaningful partnership and positive things happening."

Danny is always a believer of relationships and listens for the right opportunity to make a valuable introduction. Through a random connection on LinkedIn he met an interesting business executive with a new social venture initiative. After lengthy discussions it was obvious this person needed to meet his close friend of over 35 years. He was right! The two of them hit it off, formed a joint venture partnership, and have successfully transacted business while also impacting the world in positive ways!

"Too many people aspire to be a connector, by asking simple questions, making introductions, but not truly knowing WHY the introduction/s are made. Slow down, understand both parties better, and connect with intention. Give everyone a springboard for success. Networking, just for networking, can often backfire for you."

IT'S THE DETAILS THAT MATTER - JEFF TUTOR

Always leveling up, and strengthening top-tier relationships, Jeff knows that prioritizing is a key component to developing them. "I focus on quality over quantity, using a strong filter to measure every new introduction."

Utilizing a process to ensure the quality is as high as possible, he likes to engage in an agreement format, even if the relationships begin organically. "It's important to substantiate that those I work with are open, accessible and at an ownership/

equity level. If it's not in my wheelhouse I don't spend time on it."

Lots of people never figure out their purpose and are often time wasters to others. Our greatest asset, it needs to be managed carefully. Says Jeff, "It's priceless, and needs to be managed carefully. With each new relationship we identify expectations and outcomes for the benefit of both."

Jeff is always connecting people to their goals and dreams with his relationship capital. "I really want to see them win." Last year, he closed one deal for a client, and it's led to seven more that are in the works. Below are some of his best tips:

- Don't procrastinate. Age has nothing to do with how fast you move.
- Think exponentially, and not how people tell you to grow. Don't get comfortable.
- Don't over promise and underdeliver.
- If you can't do something, tell people the truth.
- What I don't like about email is that each correspondence creates a new one. It's just the opposite with WhatsApp.

IT'S WHO KNOWS AND TRUSTS YOU - TODD E. BENSON

Carefully crafting a network of more than 5,000 executives over the years, Todd has access that most would dream of. Serving on the boards of six companies, he is often approached for strategic introductions. "People typically reach out to me as I'm known as someone who can help create value out of opportunity and more importantly, to transfer trust."

His relationships are organized at the 5-15-50-150 level. It's been built from the companies he builds, the non-profit boards he serves, specialty business groups, and other long-term business relationships. Each is given special attention. The smaller the group and the more unique the shared passion and/or reason for connection, the more mindshare and effort committed. Beyond that, Todd also maintains contact with another 500+ in his network.

"As a product, I am a bit of a human marketplace for intellectual and financial capital. Every day I ask myself what can *only Todd* do as this is how I maximize my impact, value and contribution."

Some of his best advice/tips include:

- Connect dots and people - become known as being one who can help others create value out of ideas and opportunity and transfer trust.
- Ask yourself, why does your phone ring? What question are you the answer to? In what way(s) does the world perceive your personal brand/value / areas of differentiated value/skills/expertise?
- Look for ways to build scalability into your efforts - network at a "one to many" level. It allows you to extend your reach and makes you more efficient.
- Be generous with your time, energy and Rolodex with others when they need it most - e.g., during transition - and with respect to that which matters most to them in life - e.g., mentoring a son or daughter.

QUOTES

"A friendly 'no' is the most powerful word in the world. Its sincerity will go miles." - *Jeff Tutor*

"Be good to people. Meet people. Be there for people, and they will be there for you." - *TJ Rives*

"Be intentional about follow up. Life gets busy, and people get busy. Stay top of mind by staying in touch, and not always just to ask for something." - *Tracy Deforge*

"Being open with relationships sets the next person up for this to be paid forward. Don't be afraid to make it happen." - *Cindy Sisson*

"Face time with people is the most valuable. Time means everything." - *Rob and Keri Stuart*

"For the past 20 years, my biggest thing has been building

relationships. It's helped to create and build my real estate career. Look for opportunities to help people. It almost always comes back." - *Jason Maniecki*

"I love being an introducer but am often disappointed when those people don't keep me updated on how the conversations go." - *Scott Buss*

"I never mind doing things for people... they sometimes feel it necessary to reciprocate the value back." - *Jason Ford*

"I send video messages for people's birthday to everyone! It means so much more than an email, a text or a birthday card." - *Scott MacGregor*

"It takes lots of energy and effort to maintain relationships." - *Aaron Walker*

"Let others know you appreciate them by taking the time to build a relationship." - *Jerry Conti*

"My biggest challenge is processing the network after. When you try to engage after, a high percentage will not stay in touch. 20/80 rule. I manage on the top level and delegate the remainder to someone you can TRUST." - *Alice McLaughlin*

"My phone does not ring as much as it used to. I still start with a phone call. It's because of the longevity of my relationships." - *Andy Andrus*

"People are not good at monetizing their own networks for their own good. Do this by having lunch with someone. There is an amazing depth that can be achieved from breaking bread." - *Hany Syed*

"Spend more time building genuine relationships, and less time with people who are transaction focused." - *LaVonne Idlette*

"The most important task of networking is what happens after. Follow up and follow through is paramount." - *Enzo di Taranto*

CHAPTER FOUR

"Build a diverse network. Don't make it look and sound like you." - *David Homan*

KEEP IT SOCIAL - CHRIS CHANEY

An icon in the industry, Chris has seen business networking platforms continue to evolve over the years. Once the host of the Ivy Sport Symposium, he annually brought upwards of 600 executives together. Now his social media platforms allow that to happen daily and without an end.

"I have enjoyed LinkedIn, setting my account as a creator so anyone can follow me. If you are fairly active, it's easy to increase your visibility. By liking others' posts and content, it gives you greater visibility across the overall network. The more you engage the better LinkedIn is to serve you by surfacing the most relevant articles, posts, potential new connections, and even events It's basically my daily news."

A strong user of the platform, Chris knows that LinkedIn has unlimited opportunity. "It's a good tool to assess new opportunities and relationships. Sometimes I proactively reach out to others, and sometimes I'm asked to connect too."

"People are too dismissive of LinkedIn and new connection requests, perhaps because they get spammed. Don't be too quick to validate someone from a quick glance at their profile. You have no idea what a person is truly working on, simply by what is written." Most of his connections tend to be very thoughtful and high quality. They come from years of knowing others, and what he's looking for.

WhatsApp has become a critical tool in his arsenal. "I have over 1000 conversations across one-on-one and group chats. It's become an amazing communication platform. Informal, the app still feels personal. And it's instant! For him WhatsApp has become the most valuable tool on the business side.

"Social media helps to keep me updated on what people are working on, making tactical decisions easier. While it's important to focus on quality relationships, it is equally important to keep all of your interactions positive."

KEEPING IT REAL! - STEPHYNIE MALIK

A global leader in strategy, Stephynie is always around powerful executives. At a conference many years ago, an executive suggested she start taking questions from the audience and video the answers for social media platforms so she may widen her reach. "I really didn't want to be part of the noise. Who wants to give advice to no one and everyone at the same time? Also, who really cares about my opinion?"

Stephynie happily complied and the next day she had 1,000 messages. "All I said in the interviews was, thank you for taking the time to listen." Stephynie thought she had blown it. She had not asked anyone to like, follow or comment. From that experience, she decided to invest heavily to grow her presence and brand. It was a huge bust. No matter what expert or how much money she spent, nothing worked.

Organically, and very slowly her social media footprint grew. And then the pandemic hit.

Home one day with her oldest daughter, laughter broke out. "Mom, you have over 12,000 unread messages on Instagram!" Clearly her daughter knew something Stephynie did not and encouraged her to start posting more videos showing her vulnerability and authenticity.

"That May and June, I posted every day and kept it real." Stephynie's videos were raw, and not for everyone. "I showed real uncut excerpts from my daily life." Stephynie was getting tired of restating childhood memories or horror stories in the office. This sounded more like a whiny cat than a positive message of impact and change! Many of those who commented were not nice, but she still answered each one. "Not everything was rainbows and unicorns, some people were nasty, hurtful and even scary!"

In the aftermath, she had 5.6 million views on one video. Another got over 7 million. 55,000 comments were received. People were paying attention. Now Stephynie has over 113,000 followers on LinkedIn. And why? Because she was keeping it real!

KEY TO THE WORLD - ALEX THOMPSON

Growing up in Costa Rica, Alex knew the importance of meeting credible people. Seeing the number of foreigners visiting the country, he decided to enter this market and help them do business.

"Prior to social media, it was important to meet others face to face to develop relationships." And then the internet took hold in the country, changing everything. Says Alex, "It exposed me to additional tools to network. So, we decided to be very aggressive, promote our practice, and grow outside of Costa Rica."

Serving the travel, technology and legal space his firm has quickly expanded across Europe and North America. "Joining select organizations gave us visibility and helped to validate who we wanted to build relationships with."

Alex has visited over twenty countries and sought out lawyers with a similar focus. "We met with many executives through warm introductions. A key to success is to be strongly referred to by a trusted relationship. This helps business come easier."

His firm has now entered its 100th country. "We have a team of business developers (usually young lawyers) who understand each market. Our staff is fully bi-lingual, as each country speaks either English or Spanish."

Moving forward, Alex knows that social media tools will help to power success. "We rely on Instagram and Tik Tok to spread our message, utilizing influencers." And with the addition of email and WhatsApp, the firm maintains solid communication.

"You can have a great idea, but it's only 1% of the success of a business. Really think about how you want to connect to others. The importance of knowing the right people provides the right opportunities."

KING OF THE CASTLE - MARC JARRETT

Living in the United Kingdom, Marc Jarrett has always been networking. After a successful career in the telecom industry, he was soon introduced to WhatsApp. It boasts over two-billion users worldwide and is the most popular messaging platform. Four years later, Marc is one of the world's foremost experts in the industry.

His first exposure to WhatsApp came through Thomas Power, the UK's most prolific networker. "I was a member of his WhatsApp groups and onboarded more people than everyone else combined. But my proactive nature got me evicted five times (one of them because I posted a picture of the Dukes of Hazard). And every time I left, the network became "quiet." So, they always invited me back."

Soon, Marc was running his own group called The Virtual International Pub. It started to grow organically, when two people in the education sector started talking. Four years later, he now runs 250 groups, with nearly 200,000 participants.

"My goal is to introduce anyone to anyone. By helping people, I put myself in the position to make money throughout these groups. Like everyone, I sometimes have down days. The network never stops working ... even if I do."

LET THE MUSIC PLAY - RUSSELL RIEGER

For most of his life, Russell has been around the music industry. Starting in the 80's, he managed bands then moved on to run two different music labels. Says Russell, "In our business, trust is everything."

The industry continues to evolve, and old-school tactics only go so far. "I think it takes a while for the new school to understand what trust is. I think there is a thirst for authenticity, especially in the Tik Tok world."

During the pandemic, his life shifted dramatically to a virtual one. Committed to do whatever it takes to communicate, he remains accessible on all platforms. "I've met more people during Covid than I would have met staying in the city. (Zoom has been an extraordinary vehicle.) It's exponentially grown my network more than any other time in my life."

A believer that deep conversations can be held online, Russell treats it like a TV screen. "You can be vulnerable and open, but also protected. It's a true time compression and increases relational capital."

Knowing it's a whole new world, he continues to expand his footprint on social media, and teaches his clients along the way. "LinkedIn is my receptacle. Now I'm focused on acquiring music IP." Always on the artist's side, Russell helps them to better understand their relationship capital. "There is no better education than having been a manager, living the way the artist lives. When they get paid, you get paid."

LIGHTING THE CANDLE - TIFFANY SMITH

A friend and colleague of mine (Demetrius Brown) always says these two quotes and he lives by them - "Your Network equals your Net Worth " and "No candle lost its light by lighting another candle." These quotes really resonate with me as they are so simple, and so true yet we don't follow them. I think understanding your network and being able to work with like-minded people and build with them is amazing. Utilizing your resources and being able to be a resource and a light to someone else, that is what it is all about. Lighting someone else's light only makes your light brighter and stronger, never dim.

MIRACLE ON THE HUDSON - DAVE SANDERSON

Most everyone remembers the day. For Dave, it was an event that changed the course of his life forever. "I'll be forever grateful. The lesson I learned from that day is that it's all about perseverance, resilience, and mindset."

From the plane, there is one person I interact with every couple of months (we went to the same hospital). He was the first one out; I was the last passenger out. A year after "the miracle on the Hudson," they got together and sponsored a luncheon to thank New Jersey's responders for everything they had done. He met 60-70% of the people in attendance. He knows everyone who went out on the right side of the plane and several who went out on the left side that ultimately went to the NY shore.

Dave is always there to help bridge the relationship value between passengers and airlines and is often called to speak after a major transportation incident. "When Delta invited me to speak to the flight attendants' school, the audience wanted to know what *really* happened (not what you saw on TV or the movie)."

Dave started working with the Red Cross a few months after the incident. At first, he was speaking at local churches and telling his story. "The CEO of the American Red Cross in Charlotte heard about it and asked me to Keynote an upcoming fundraising event." That announcement almost doubled the room attendance. He was soon asked to speak at a national event, and the relationship with the Red Cross took off.

It's been fourteen years now, and Dave still gives platelets. One of the biggest things that have come out of the Miracle on the Hudson for Dave is that he can go to any state in the country and have a connection through this relationship.

MY ONE THING - DEREK CHAMPAGNE

As far back as Derek can remember, he was networking. The parents of part-time touring musicians, his fondest memories included being on stage by the age of three and watching his parents interact with the audience.

Perhaps the world's youngest band manager (age 12), he was booking "gigs" across a tri-state area. Building meaningful relationships was key to booking return gigs. "When the internet came out, I was so excited. It was so much easier!" said Derek. And a favorite trick for an early business was following the Sunday morning paper route and sliding his own flyers into each after they were delivered.

Now networking has become focused, purposeful, rewarding. "Every year I share my 'One Thing' video to my top 100 relationships. When you think of me this year, only think of me for this one thing that I need to accomplish. It helps to align my vision with the entire network." For Derek, this tactic recently led to the successful expansion of three new territories for his company. And it took only three conversations within his trusted network to finalize each partner.

Below are some of Derek's favorite principals:

- Collaboration is key. Share what you have generously and always be a student in learning from others.
- My network is reserved for high level, good people coming together, just for the sake of helping each other.
- Grow together. It's a shortcut, and will save you decades of mistakes.
- Help promote others without expectation of reciprocity, and it will help promote you.
- It always has to do with how you are perceived and positioned in your network. Always show up as a valuable resource and you will always get passed on as a highly trusted opportunity.
- Partner right, network right and the results can happen immediately.
- The exponential value of helping someone else comes back time after time.
- The older I get, the more impatient I get for outcomes. I surround myself with leaders who value their time as much as I do.

OLD SCHOOL - JULIUS JACKSON

At the ripe young age of 75, many are in awe of the energy Julius exhibits. With regular trips to Africa, he continues to show all of us why relationships mean everything.

"I don't see any downside to being socially active online," says Julius. "I do utilize some tools on occasion (i.e. Microsoft Teams), but don't use Tik Tok or Zoom when discussing sensitive information, as many technology platforms are not secure enough." He likes to move information by WhatsApp and in person, because of the level of business associated with it. "Be yourself and be very nice. Always listen. You will learn more by observing."

Having been blessed with interpreters when in foreign countries from long standing relationships in Government allows Julius to network seamlessly. He will utilize Google Translator as part of the process when needed. "I was surprised how long it took others to understand the business processes but have now added it to my working timeline. To me it means capitalizing on what's in the environment, especially humans. This relates to products that we create, helping you move closely to the business you set."

As for the next generation, he continues to press forward.

"When I'm trying to communicate with younger folks, it's very difficult for them to accept the fact that our experiences and challenges are honest teaching lessons. Network discrimination still happens. But if you move forward diligently and with care, things can still get done."

PERCEPTION VS. REALITY - FRED BEAN

Looking for a better summer job after college, Fred got into the travel industry by accident. "My roommate knew I was having difficulty. I hated it and called in sick as much as possible. He convinced me to come to Hyatt, which had a call center. I took the job, as it combined my love for technology and integration around hospitality and tourism."

Through the years Fred continued to move up the ranks. "I read a passage in a book that said to find a task that's being neglected and own it. I did it and became an expert." He started managing teams. "Instead of sitting at my desk, I was always on the floor talking to the team. I cared, they cared, and we excelled with results."

Networking is a daily exercise for Fred. "To manage relationships across fourteen different time zones, I utilize many messaging tools. Not a lot of thought goes into it; some relationships are more active than others. There is no real science to the process," Fred said.

"I'm a big believer that what you put out there needs to be careful and persistent. Authenticity is important, especially in hospitality and entertainment." With his networks blended, sometimes he has to be careful not to overlap them. "Some relationships started as friends and moved to business and vice versa."

For Fred, showing up is 90% of his success. "Make yourself available. Be mindful of the right opportunities. You can't say yes to everything. Be aggressive. Don't let someone tell you that a goal can't be achieved. And keep moving forward."

QUOTES

"A lot of organizations now offer online networking, but don't feel it's working. Even if they connect on the App prior to, it doesn't often lead to a face-to-face (was truly a wasted effort). A bad example of "White Noise'." - *Alice McLaughlin*

"Am a very direct parent, talk to them like they are grown. I know what we are dealing with. Teaching lessons about Bots, not sending DM's, not posting things that you don't want others to see down the road. Keeping it clean. Always knowing someone else will see, hear and respond to what is going to social media." - *Elisabeth Flach*

"Be memorable and bring value first." - *Amanda Catarzi*

"For years, MJ starts each day by posting a positive message on her Facebook profile (I look forward to them myself). Her personal philosophy has been to always highlight the good and stay away from conflicting comments. "It's everyone's choice how they use social media. For me, I enjoy sharing positive sayings and uplifting news." - *MJ Pedone*

"Ghosting is a huge pet peeve. If I've taken the time to arrange a meeting, call, follow up, etc. it shows disrespect. If I miss a meeting or have to cancel, it makes me want to provide additional value to the person. If someone misses a meeting with me before a negotiation, it often helps to give me a better position." - **Jason Ford**

"I am constantly learning and adapting to how I can better use social media, and then amplify with earned media interviews to magnify my efforts. It's helped me to extend my reach and to make a positive impression on others." - **Darrin Gray**

"I have been extolling the virtues of virtual networking for several years now. It's clean and leaves no carbon footprint. It's free, since the internet has become an essential utility which we all pay for anyway. It saves a ton of time and money. But perhaps best of all is its globality – the world really is our oyster when it comes to growing our tribes and meeting new people." - **Marc Jarrett**

"I think there is a big gap in the reliance of tech to provide socialization and interpersonal communities. Ownership is always the best model of having a great life." - **Carrie Nikitin**

"Introductions need to be made carefully. One bad one can have horrible repercussions." - **Drew Sheinman**

"In the virtual world, how do you know if someone is paying attention?" - **Kiana**

"LinkedIn is the best way to share your voice and connect in an authentic way." - **Jason Kolker**

"One of my pet peeves is how people utilize LinkedIn. You accept the request, and the next second they send me a pitch. No effort made to develop communication whatsoever. Not my thing." - **Fred Bean**

"The world has changed, and social media is a huge part of that." - **Ian O'Donnell**

"Try to teach the kids how to get established on Twitter, as it's where the coaches look. They all have a brand." -*Josh Folds*

"Walk (physically or virtually) into the majority of situations with the mindset that you may be able to connect the person(s) you're speaking with to someone else who will be an asset. That's the key to networking, and to making yourself more valuable (if not invaluable). It will be repaid, without question." - *Diane Byrne*

"We are in an era, particularly for kids, where forcing face to-face conversation is critical. It's an uphill battle with the overwhelming power of social media channels and the ease of their use. Fight the technology and get back to the basics of human interaction." - *Rob Vaka*

"Zoom opened up the ability for global presentations but diminished the networking. Collapsed the distance for people but expanded the conversation length." - *Stephen Meade.*

CHAPTER FIVE

"Don't succumb to the fear of missing out. Not all invitations to network have value. Assess each, and make sure they align with your current goals." - Gina Scott

PIECES OF THE PUZZLE - KEN HUBBARD

A true master of business communication, Ken has always been careful with how he manages the process. For him, it's truly important to find areas of commonality when starting a conversation.

But no matter how hard you try, sometimes it's just not a fit. As he says, "It's not Jenga."

"Get to know the other person, share with them tidbits of advice or offer to make an introduction. Do it without expecting something in return. Put a time limit on when you would like a return gesture. It could be as simple as them making a suggestion on when to play golf."

If your need to finish a business goal is shorter, then begin to lean on the person for help. "It's like a statue," says Ken," You start with a chip, and you end with a sculpture. It's not instant gratification. Getting to know someone doesn't happen overnight."

A great example came from years ago, when a CTO of a Hollywood Movie Production studio asked him to increase their contract by a few million dollars. It took Ken three months to realize that the person he didn't want to deal with was making the decisions. And after that, it was another three to get a 15-minute appointment, which turned into five minutes. "I delivered an efficient proposal, to the point, and with solutions. But it did help to secure business. Even though I didn't like him, and he wasn't nice, I made modifications in my delivery and got the business."

READING BETWEEN THE LINES - CHARLES BAKER

Listening is a key skill in all areas of life. And while networking, it often supplies context not easily seen. For this worldly lawyer, reading between the lines has proven its value time and time again.

Frequently lecturing to law school students, Charles often discusses the term *networking*. "I don't like the word. It has a shallow perspective. I view this model as connections that are a mile wide and an inch deep. Don't network for the sake of networking. Establish genuine connections. Be authentic. Take time to listen to someone. Listen to and understand their story."

Charles could be sitting on a plane, or in a business meeting. But he's always focused on doing the right thing. "I spend lots of time on email, text and WhatsApp just to stay in front of people, but my genuine connections are live, and I'm interested in them. My process is informal. My business is primarily referred by existing clients and both personal and professional relationships."

One such story came when meeting an NBA team owner who was positioning to sell his professional sports franchise. "Our conversation quickly turned to parenting, and I recommended a book to read. This gesture was well received, as two years later I got a call back to help make a sale. We have since become very close friends." What comes around, goes around!

RELATIONSHIP CAPITAL - HANY SYED

Want to build amazing wealth with your network and develop true relationship capital? For Hany, it comes down to three key things: Invest in your network, expand your sphere, maintain and monetize key relationships.

Invest in Your Network

In key conversations, always ask, "How can I help?"

Invest in the relationship very early. Put time into getting to know others. Some will last, some won't. It's Ok to Move on. "I'm a very open networker, doing it just because it's right. It's a strong trait that I believe in. Once you are in the circle, you are in. It's bad on you if you don't operate this way."

In person. Zoom. Text. WhatsApp for International. "Remain flexible," says Hany. "Use the channel that the other person likes."

Expand Your Sphere

It's always been about expanding my networks strategically. Whether Dubai or Silicon Valley, things seemed to merge naturally. Stay open to our global shift and continue networking.

"I can get to most anyone these days. Now I just have to be specific about who I want to meet, and my network will respond. It's up to me to do this work and get an outcome."

Maintain and Monetize Key Relationships

Try to stay in touch with people. Send out a monthly update email to my network. Zoom has been massive. It allows true friendships to be built. It's much better than nothing.

Hany created a Founders community with Columbia of other VC's. Around 200 companies are invited. It's action oriented, customer facing and focused on best practices. Each participant has to be introduced to be accepted.

"With the depth of my relationships and the fact that this vertical is quite fraternal, it's allowed for escalated growth (unlike the education sector). I now have over forty advisors, with even bigger Rolodexes that have allowed me to monetize these relationships."

I don't just take calls. If I pick up the phone, it's important to me.

RELATIONSHIPS MATTER MOST - AARON WALKER

In 2010, Aaron was ready to retire. But like many successful entrepreneurs, he was soon pulled back in. "I never thought I would create a Mastermind. However, after attending a well-known local mastermind for more than a decade I became aware of the massive value of meeting weekly with unbiased, trusted advisors.

From there the momentum grew, his friends could see the value that Aaron added as a life and business coach from his 30-plus year journey as a very successful entrepreneur. Big A, as his friends call him, soon became a podcast guest to share his life experiences. Aaron initially had no idea what that was or any experience as a guest. After that initial interview Aaron was surprised to land 15 one-on-one clients. This was the catalyst to launch his first mastermind. He originally told his wife that he would only host that *one* group.

The interviews continued, and soon Big A had enough executives for two additional groups. Robin, peering over her glasses, shaking her head said, "Here we go again," Robin had been down this path many times before living with an entrepreneur.

"Successful men find themselves making decisions in a vacuum. It's lonely at the top. We offer the men an environment that allows for vulnerability and transparency. The groups become more than business. It's safe and unbiased. Deep levels of trust are created, and each man can share his trials, and seek ways to offer support in a very real way."

Iron Sharpens Iron Mastermind today hosts 150 men in groups of 10.

Big A has a couple of core foundational principles that will serve everyone well. "Be accurate when you share what you have done, where you have been, and what you want to accomplish. Don't be arrogant, be truthful with a great amount of humility. Don't condemn or pass judgement, be a friend and an awesome resource. You don't earn the right to call someone on the carpet until you have spent time with them." Aaron believes men need accountability, encouragement, resources, networking, and genuine raw feedback. We were created to be in community."

His general networking philosophy is simple. "I don't follow the traditional model of only calling someone when I need something. I firmly believe we should regularly call friends, family and colleagues to have a conversation with no ask." Big A continues, "Be truly interested in the person. People only remember how you make them feel. Forge a real relationship by making them feel important ... because they are."

SHARP DRESSED MAN - ALAN PAVLOSKY, CO-FOUNDER

All Sports United was starting to gain momentum, and our access to the professional sports sector continued to grow. As we launched new events, and a national awards platform, an interesting conversation began to unfold. The Trunk Club, a specialty division of Nordstrom's, wanted to become a corporate partner. In return for strategically connecting them at a series of events, they agreed to provide custom clothing to my business partner and me. It was a great example of how your network can pay off, and we still own a nice wardrobe!

SHOW UP TO WIN! - KENNY HAZLETT

With a longtime career in the motorsports industry, Kenny knows all about preparation. "Just like an athletic competition, it's so important to write out your goals for any event you are engaging in."

He went on to say, "Working in an industry like this, you sometimes feel like you are in a box. The good news is that I'm well connected with deep relationships."

"To have longevity in anything you do is really hard. Competition never goes away. Things happen so quickly, so fluidly. Your personality and your word equal your reputation. If I promise to do something, then it will be completed. It's amazing how many don't follow through."

Always a runner, Kenny first found out about ultra trail running on social media. "It was an event I always wanted to do. So, I went online and eventually found the community."

"When you are running a trail in the middle of nowhere it's a surreal experience (mind, heart, soul). The competition pace feeds you." With the high-level events, Kenny knew there were only so many spots available. "I had to go old school, get out my pen, and draft letters to the organizing committee and my US Senator." His efforts paid off, as Kenny secured spots in upcoming races.

Kenny sacrificed his weekends to train for the Mont Blanc competition in France (over the French Alps). "I was always preparing for runs that Saturday and Sunday and would drive 2 1/2 hours into the mountains of Virginia to do a five-hour run to gain altitude." The first American male over fifty to even compete in Mont Blanc, Kenny has also made the podium in one race and now has two Senior Olympics on his resume.

"Even in sports you have to network. My daughter and I went over five days earlier to France, partly for training. While there I utilized my networking background to engage with local experts to better understand the racecourse, elements of the day, and additional logistical needs/issues."

SOMEWHERE IN THE MIDDLE OF NOWHERE - SASHA LUND

Only by asking will you know where Sasha is on any given day. This week it was to travel to a small town in Texas, a ski resort in Switzerland, and a beach in Cyprus. "My travels are always a combination of business and life."

Being a person who lives on a plane has allowed her to engage in genuine conversations. "You need to actually care, and not do it just to do it." To keep the relationships going is a challenge when traveling so much, so Sasha always sends a correspondence or phone call during a special time in another person's life.

Carefully watching the next generation, Sasha is well aware that this demographic tires from the old school mentality of dressing up, working from a certain location and during certain hours. This leads to more spontaneous video calls, often not in a work environment. For her, it helps to add to the authenticity of the relationship.

Hosting an intimate dinner one night, she invited 10 different people from 10 different countries. Not your average gathering, it included several Heads of State, influential business executives and high net worth family members. "Each brought a dish from their culture and helped us all experience where everyone was from. What I have come to realize through my journey is that people are attracted to people. How you communicate often helps to bring certain individuals toward each other."

TAKING IT BACK TO THE OLD SCHOOL - AL REYNOLDS

A product of the banking world on Wall Street, Al learned early on the importance of networking. "My influencers were CPAs, family offices, and lawyers. Building relationships over time helped me gain the trust to be referred to key individuals."

For Al, technology is raising the bar and giving him a front-row seat to industry "best practices." He's a heavy user of LinkedIn and relies on its speed of access and depth of knowledge to uncover new opportunities. "During Covid, the proliferation of discussions was unprecedented. And it supplied an opportunity to make connections far beyond other methods."

But he knows you still must talk to people, as technology and social media will only take you so far. "If I find someone who has parallel interests and reciprocal opportunities, I'll set up an introductory meeting. Back in the day, it had to be face-to-face. Nowadays you can get on Zoom with someone from Asia or Europe, and it's been a huge change in access."

Still old school, Al likes to be in a room and feel the energy. Recently he moved to Los Angeles to do more TV work and he often heads now to charitable events, lunches, premieres and panel discussions. It's an investment of time that will help to start relationships. He's also brought back the dinner party model. "Breaking bread provides a human connection with the business touch."

THE 37TH PARALLEL - JEFFREY MENAGED

The private aviation community is a small one, and because of that relationships are of tremendous value. Add to that the pandemic, and every friendship's value continues to increase in value.

"One of the tricks I have found to be most useful is that your luck comes from giving. Basics are important: be presentable, have something to say, know how to get into a room. People are most responsive when you help them any way you can. I had a client who was a collector of campaign buttons. I was at an antique store and bought a big bag of buttons. The client was overwhelmed with happiness. He responded like the bag had money in it.

The industry requires unique access for the clients, which doesn't allow Jeff to create a schedule. "Because of this, I like to have a short list of what needs to be accomplished and push other things out. When trying to accomplish less, I actually get more done." He's also a big believer in using the phone as much as possible.

"I think what people respond to the most is thoughtfulness. If you go out of your way, just to show you know about them, it goes far."

THE ART OF CONVERSATION - EMIL LUTH

At the early age of 17, Emil grabbed his skateboard and headed to San Francisco. Having grown up in Denmark, and being fiercely curious, this adventure has proven to be one of many. And it led to a strong desire to interact with as many interesting individuals as he could.

Thanks to 10 years of martial arts experience, (Karate, 1st Dan Black Belt), Emil has a level of perspective that few understand. "I can see so much across a room, and it includes body language. I want to network at the highest possible level, as this training has helped me to do so."

In his early 20s, Emil worked many large-scale events involving celebrities and executives. It helped him understand others and improve his gift of gab. "I attend as many dinners, private events, and VIP functions as I can. It's where I shine."

No nonsense by default, Emil has always focused on the "art of limitation." He knows that it's more important to have quality relationships than a huge database. "Networking can often be over-consumption. I've carefully crafted my network through various business verticals and work hard to manage each relationship."

With a global perspective, he's developed a truly unique skill set. "I can understand when people speak the same language and know what's being said between the lines. With my global experience, and cultural background, I have tremendous skills in matchmaking others for the right reason." One such story happened at a dinner in Zurich. "The room was populated by some real powerful individuals, and I felt out of my depth. But that night I said I was the highlight of the dinner because of my energy, authenticity and how I could help bridge conversations."

QUOTES

"Advice to those starting out - Do it. It's necessary. No man/ woman is an island. Collaboration can only happen through networking." - *Alycia Powell*

"Always show up early. It's better to know what you are getting into." - *Kenny Hazlett*

"Always try to find something to make you stand out." - *Cindy Sisson*

"Ask for permission, whether it's a hug or a handshake." - *Samantha Katz*

"Be careful when determining which events will provide a true return on effort." - *Fred Bean*

"Be insanely authentic." - **Drew Sheinman**

"Check your ego at the door. There are other people out there with better expertise." - **Dave Sanderson**

"Everyone has a process of interacting. People get there when they're ready." - **Alan Pavlosky**

"Find something uncommon that you have in common." - **Todd Benson**

"If there is no chemistry, don't drag things out. Move on." - **Didi Wong**

"Keep it real. Ask good questions. Be authentic and genuinely interested." - **Seth Buechley**

"My goal is to find my who's for my how's." - **Dave Sanderson**

"One-way networkers. Be wary of these executives. They often brag about big networks, drop names, and seem excited to make introductions. But they never do." - **Scott Buss**

"Something I have learned is to network with others who have similar visions and moral ethical compasses. I like to find others who are driven by more than just money, those who want to help others and leave a positive mark on the world. That's who I want to work with. One of my good friends and best networker I thought was broke when I first met him. I tried to help him for free with a business he had, thinking he was in hard times when I met him. I eventually found out he was the most connected person (especially in sports and entertainment) that I had ever met and an amazing human being." - **Jeff Turk**

"There needs to be a book about it. Been to many conferences. Speaking to people to "listen to experts," most leave being more confused. Pump in comfortable energy into the conversation. Take the time to match the right people to each other." - **Andy Andrus**

"The upside is that in general, men do not consider us competition. It's changing, but very slowly. Professional flirting is often done. Tall and attractive women can often be intimidating. Learning how to use your traits can have an enhanced benefit to overall networking. I was in a conversation with a group of men, where someone tried to move me out physically, a good friend brought me back in." - **Nancy May**

"When I meet with people, I do my best to understand what's truly important to the person and try to help wherever I can. Most often, the response is of surprise because it's not often asked. It doesn't cost much to be a resource. The universe works in mysterious ways." - **Luciane Serifovic**

CHAPTER SIX

"LinkedIn is a tool that I leverage. It helps me to share knowledge and become a subject matter expert. It's really about being active in the spaces where people who think like me will be." - *Rebecca Longawa*

THE BEST IN CLASS - JULIE SCHMIDT HASSON

A lifelong teacher, Julie always had a passion to help others, and support the industry as a whole. When she started working her focus was research oriented. Trained in qualitative data, her curiosity started to fuel a new goal. After many interviews, and gathering needed data, she started to share her story in blogs. "I never had a plan. It all just snowballed. Soon I was on stage giving a Ted Talk." This led to her video receiving over 100,000 views.

Julie's greatest lesson is to be honest. And a favorite place to engage in meaningful discussions is on Twitter. "In the education space there is honesty in short tweets. Almost like a camaraderie." Diving deeper into the subject, she shared even more. "Twitter is not invasive and allows me to convey my message. It can come from an instant thought, and often supplies an instant response."

THE BIGGEST WINNER - JIM GEMANAKOS

While watching Season 4 of NBC's The Biggest Loser, I watched the "Weight Loss Twins" win the show. Their story touched my heart, and soon Jim Germanakos and I had connected through MySpace.

It was 2008, and I immediately invited both Bill and Jim to join me in Phoenix for some events during Super Bowl Week (one of which I hosted). They were THE HIT of the week, as the show was a huge success. Bill and Jim spent the week walking red carpet events, being interviewed, and asked to attend multiple parties.

We have remained good friends, and some of Jim's networking wisdom appears throughout this book. I'm thankful that MySpace allowed us to connect!

Instagram Hostage

It's not all good. More often than not we hear of accounts being frozen, deleted, and sometimes held for ransom. Recently, a friend of mine received an anonymous text, only to find out that if they wanted to get their account back it would cost $400. After many emails, and hours of disappointment, the account was deleted by Instagram. Sadly, my friend lost all their content and had to start again from scratch.

The Principal's Office

We all can think back to our days in school, and what it meant to be called into the office. But for a newly hired schoolteacher, this had a whole new meaning. As an accomplished collegiate gymnast, this young lady had a significant social media footprint. Thousands of photos and videos were on a variety of her social media accounts. But in accepting her job to teach she found out that everything had to go. Nearly six hours later, the process was done, and the job started.

The Singing Bodyguard

This is the kind of story that movies are made of. Jim is an accomplished law enforcement professional and an amazing singer of Sinatra songs. His "side hustle" once put him alongside a well-known billionaire who heard of this talent, and asked Jim to sing at a private event. Almost 10 years later, the two have become great friends and enjoy many adventures together.

THE BRAND INNOVATORS - BRANDON GUTMAN AND MARC STERNBERG

A true success story in networking, Brandon started out like many. He read everything he could, attended many events, and honed his skills in sales and business development.

It's all about *who knows you*," says Brandon. "You must become discoverable, where people will reach out to you." He started writing a byline/weekly article for a few trade magazines. This quickly elevated to writing for *Fast Company* and *Forbes*. It turned out to be the inception of Brand Innovators, in written form.

Brand Innovators was created to help brand marketers meet each other. Brandon soon teamed up with Marc Sternberg and they turned it into a business. "Early on, there were many wannabes. It's not that others can't attempt to do this, but few are willing to take the risk, the time, and the effort for long-term success."

Brandon and Marc knew that it would take an immense effort to scale their company, which was the culmination of nearly 35 years of combined business experience. "It's not something that can be created just by placing money into it. It has taken years of relationship capital, time and investment in each individual." Now in its 11th year, Brand Innovators boasts over 50 employees, more than 200 sponsors and beyond 50,000 community members.

THE BUSINESS OF SPORTS - CHARLES KIM

Starting in the investment banking sector, Charles never expected to one day run a company with a focus in China. Working in South Korea in the early 2000s, his eyes opened like the matrix. He knew that this consumer market was like nothing the world had ever seen.

"I wanted to better understand how to make this market profitable. As I once raised private equity for many of China's most powerful social media platforms, my relationships became quite strong with the founders of each."

Charles saw the powerful opportunity between athletes and product, but he didn't know anyone in the market. The market loved sports. In particular they enjoy basketball, soccer and any personality from entertainment. With no network, he turned to his Family Office relationships. "One of my peers was connected to a retired NBA player. This led to a phone call, and a business partnership (as the player had notoriety overseas). With validation I began to make and receive other introductions."

"Things began to move fast, and soon I was introduced to the NFL Players Association, and went to an event during Super Bowl Week in Atlanta."

Charles has worked hard to build over 100 relationships in the industry. Could be an agent, a parent or another family member. "WhatsApp is my strongest asset. I utilize it for team conversations (meaning anyone involved in the athletes business - agent, biz manager, family member, etc.). It gives us real-time feedback and updates. Even the older participants can use it."

THE CARING CONNECTOR - NANCY MAY

For over 30 years I have helped others network. Oftentimes it went without a return of effort. Many relationships are superficial. I am more than willing to open a door, but I'm hoping the gesture will one day be returned.

My dad once asked me, "you know everybody. How did you learn to do this"? I said, "Dad, I learned from you." He was a designer of eyeglass frames for many famous people. Our vacations were industry conventions. I would go and carry baskets of cheese and wine to thank my customers. *Be good to the people who are good to you.* This is where I learned to start networking.

Today it's CRM, it's customer lists, it's not relationships. But you profit more by keeping a small group of individuals tight. As long as you stay in touch, and never forget, the relationship will remain strong. Bad people will remain bad people. "Morals" can have a different meaning for everyone. But from biz/networking, it's very easy to tell who a good person is.

I still teach clients how to network. I had a Fortune 500 CEO call me one day and asked to introduce me to a colleague. She was leaving the company, had no network, and needed to build one. This came because the focus had always been *inside* the company. Entrepreneurs and salespeople have to have broad, diverse and deep networks across all verticals.

THE GARAGE SALE SWEETHEART - AMANDA HENGST

At the early age of seven, Amanda was already hustling. Her most fond memory comes from a community garage sale. "I had a cookie and lemonade stand. Smiles were always free." When given a $10 or $20 dollar bill, she would try to upsell each instead of giving change. But it didn't stop there.

Knowing that people come to shop, she jumped right in. "What are you looking for, and why are you here"? And to add to her enthusiastic approach, Amanda would often go to the houses nearby, ask others what they were looking for, and bring them back to her parents' garage sale.

Amanda started training in martial arts at age ten. In her early 20s, and already a Black Belt, she tried her luck at Mixed Martial Arts. "I played the sweetness card and acted shy. But when the match started, I applied my fighting skills and always won."

In one of her first jobs, Amanda worked for a meal prep company. "I was introduced to the bodybuilding world and started doing live presentations online to help sell the brand." As her career continued, she realized LinkedIn had shifted from a resume focus to strategic business focus. "It was easy for me to stand out. I excel at storytelling, have an edgy personality, and lots of tattoos. People are drawn to that."

Confident in her ability to capture people's attention, Amanda is a master of driving new business from "cold" direct messaging. "If you do it right, it can be quite effective. Once you send the message, a familiarity is already there. All my prominent connections have come from this." She goes on to say, "Always have a strategy to get into people's DMs and bring value. I give value three times before asking for anything." This intensity has led to countless new relationships that continue today.

Amanda has an impressive network from her efforts. She keeps every business card and organizes them with large clips into segments (entrepreneurs, government, law enforcement, etc.). Depending on where they are in the rotation depends on where they are in the process. And how has Amanda managed to organize and maintain her ever-growing network? "Nothing is in my head. Now I use a white board, write notes on business cards, and in notebooks."

THE CULTURE CLUB - MATT KOWALAK

At the age of 23, Matt was living in China. While there, learning how to make friends, judge business opportunities and intentions was always a challenge. Like anything new, it took time to fully understand and cultivate friendships.

"Networking means something different to everyone. Americans tend to think of it as just a place for connections of business. In China, it's so much more than relationships. It's very specific like yin and yang. It's not formal, but you must always find a way to reciprocate. There is a greater focus to repay the gesture or good fortune that came from another person's efforts."

With a global perspective, and the freedom to live anywhere, Matt has continued his travels. Most recently in Mexico and Thailand, he kept his focus on networking for business and cultivating strong relationships. Each time, he found ways to add value back.

Now Matt is in Japan. With a specific business opportunity but no network, he had to summon all of his skill sets and build a flexible plan with a team focused in the area. By activating chosen global executives to begin building the pipeline, and utilizing LinkedIn as a search engine, he has been able to build another strong circle of relationships.

"It's about understanding your resources, but also shaping the team to match the opportunity over time."

THE KEY TO ACCESS - CRAIG HANDLEY

No matter what the language, no matter where in the world, no matter what the business topic, Craig is always ready to discuss it. "I leave time in my calendar each day for random conversations. It's always good to have availability."

Often finding himself in conversations with people from other countries, he tries to be prepared by understanding how that person's country does business. "Negotiation can be very tricky as other countries like to negotiate until one party leaves the deal, then they come back after the deal is dead and accept your last offer." Craig goes on to say, "Before I knew that I felt intense pressure and my margins were so low I might as well have been their employee. Communication in other countries can tend to be more business-like, until a true relationship is created. And networking can be more complicated, as connections are often made because someone is friends, not because they are the best business resource."

While networking is universal, Craig knows that you must use the tool that the other person is comfortable with. "WhatsApp is my preferred communication tool. The response time feels quicker, and you can see if the message was read, and if someone is online.

Craig sees much happening in the Metaverse and Web3. "Streaming is crossing into the Influencer space. Some companies are starting to utilize Influencers like a Board of Advisors. It's moving at a high speed. With the Meta, stores are being stacked by influencers and moved forward with AI."

THE KNOCKOUT NETWORKER - MICHAEL GOLDBERG

Always into fitness, Michael got the boxing bug fifteen years ago. "Watching someone jump rope, I decided to approach him and ask for help to do it myself." A simple conversation led to a friendship, a lesson in boxing, and soon competitive fighting.

Nine years ago, Michael was speaking for a big client at a sales meeting. While on the stage, he started to share a boxing story (as he usually would). "I had a guy in a cowboy hat stand up and say, 'You are a knockout networker.' That day the brand name was born."

Knock Out Networking is now an industry powerhouse, guiding executives nationally and providing expert advice on the subject. And as a competitive boxer, Michael knows the best punches needed to win the fight. They are:

- Know Your Target Market - Industry, Profession, Company Names.
- Know Your Centers of Influence - Professions Serving Your Market.
- Know Your Specific "Ask" - Specific Introductions You Want.
- Know How to Be Collaborative - Focus on Helping Others.
- Know Where to Network - Location, Location, Location.

One of the true experts in networking, his advice continues. "Get your message out there and increase your connections. It will help you win the round, and the fight!"

With almost 15 years in competitive boxing, Michael continues to expand his relationships in that sector. And this year it led to an amazing invitation to a Golden Gloves event. "I probably wouldn't have gotten into this room without my tie to the sport. It's led to so many opportunities both personally and professionally." He's truly the Knockout Networker!

THE ORCHESTRATED CONNECTOR - DAVID HOMAN

On November 1st, 2017, David held his first event. Realizing his diverse network didn't know each other, he carefully constructed an invitation list of 40 close relationships. And out of this Orchestrated Connecting was born.

David Homan is a classical composer and connector. You can find his music simply by asking Alexa to play it. He's as gifted in crafting harmonies and melodies as he is in composing high-impact connections between action-oriented, natural-givers.

A community of impact-focused super-connectors whose relationship value is beyond comparison, Orchestrated Connecting continues to grow. "I built it for connectors to be valued as connectors in a few conversations, instead of a few years. It's up to each of them to *ask* for their value. Connectors are natural givers. They never question it," says David.

His organization will expand to four other cities this year, and eventually go international. And David is now finishing his book on networking methodology. "It's important to keep in mind that you will often be asked to join every initiative for which you can make a connection. You cannot always do this, and so should weigh these opportunities carefully."

"Our relationships are often the reason we are given opportunities. The role we embrace in business or philanthropy discussions centers on understanding the passions and desires of others, and whether what is being presented to you would resonate with people you know."

QUOTES

"Give first and meet others who are willing to do the same. It can lead to more than you will ever imagine." - *Jerry Conti*

"Helping others extend their reach helps you extend yours." - *Carrie Nikitin*

"I don't sell anything, but instead present. By introducing people to each other, it strengthens my profile because of this gesture. Down the road, I know the unseen value that can be provided." - *Hany Syed*

"If I don't know how to get somewhere, I always know someone who does." - *TJ Rives*

"If you are grateful first, the rest will appear." - *Kiana*

"It's not about the money, it's always about the people." - Didi Wong

"Just be nice." - *Kenny Hazlett*

"My most valuable asset is the relationship network of the people I have. Through the law of reciprocity, good things have happened. You have to be OK with a lack of it because it's about giving back, not getting." - **Rob Vaka**

"Most people who set out to be experts at networking are not going to be able to achieve the level of success they seek. It's a marathon and not a sprint." - **Brandon Gutman**

"Relationships are like gold and can't be quantified. When both parties are willing to give and help, it is the best." - **Russ Rieger**

"The one key to life is who you know, who you pour into, and who you help." - **Rob Vaka**

"Trust is the cornerstone to relationships." - **Ian O'Donnell**

"Turn whatever challenge you have into a triumph." - **Dave Sanderson**

"We often ask for advice, but it comes with general context. As relationships increase, so does the return." - **Aaron Walker**

"When you walk into a room, you should know who to speak to, who not to speak to, and when to end a conversation." - **Didi Wong**

"You'll be enriched by being available to others." - **Tracy Deforge**

CHAPTER SEVEN

"What you do is irrelevant. What you need is important." - *Stephen Meade*

THE PRAYER NETWORK - GREG SIDDERS

Relocating from California to Maine, Greg and his family went through many transitions. From warm weather to cold, from big city to small town, from West Coast culture to New England culture.

"Maine is a throwback in some ways. I came with lots of experience in social media, but it wasn't widely used here." Then the Pandemic hit. "Our church needed us, and we needed them. Live streaming helped us stay connected, share our message, and continue building relationships."

Learning from his adult children, Greg has slowly adapted to networking. "In my training it was never discussed. We were taught to be competent, but not connected." He knows that the best things happen in small groups. "The people impacted by your life are those who are actually in it."

Even today, White Pine continues to have an online option. "Many are watching," says Greg. "Those who can't be with us in-person are blessed by having this access." Communicating any way possible, he will never stop sharing. "People want friendships, and we can help foster them."

In the travel industry since 2011, Shane's mantra has always been exceptional service with a personal touch. His signature is unique vacation experiences, impact travel, and charitable support. With the creation of the Entrepreneur Travel Club, Shane can now add networking to the list.

"Travel has been underutilized in forming relationships. The time spent together on a trip cannot be duplicated. Using high quality focused time with travel helps to develop relationships through trust and commonality." This has also led to the creation of WhatsApp groups prior to the trip. Often, the attendees will maintain a connection there, long after unpacking their bags.

Each vacation trip is carefully curated, and usually comes from a partnership with a respected mastermind community. Due diligence is done on all participants, to increase the level of interaction. "In-person provides the opportunity to get to know each other better. What I've seen is when you set a good table everyone will have a good conversation. You don't have to set up the networking, just the environment."

THE PUBLIC SERVANT - RAYMOND JACKSON

Raymond enlisted in the Army right out of high school and dedicated his early adult life to serving our borders. It wasn't until his early 20s that he started his college experience. The time on campus as the "old guy" opened up a whole new world for him.

Says Raymond, "I'm an independent, in the truest sense of the world. Live and let live." His parents are first-generation Americans, coming from German occupied Holland (mother) and Jamaica (dad). They did what it took to survive, working many jobs and eventually owning some small businesses. Raymond was taught about hard work, attention to detail, and the fact that a pretty face alone won't get you very far.

The next thirty years took him and his Air Force wife (Rachel) all over the world. Rachel retired from the Air Force and began teaching Law School (he remained in the Army). "We later had the opportunity to move to Hermosa Beach, CA and loved it!" Raymond quickly embraced the community, coaching youth sports and volunteering in school all while taking a year off after retiring from the Army. That break turned into eight years.

"I was so busy. A city council member resigned his council seat and Hermosa Beach held a special election to fill his seat. A school board member suggested I run. Me and a couple folks conducted an old school campaign, and I was elected, over four other candidates." When the term ended, he was re-elected to the city council and was later elected to the Mayoral position.

Social media ended up playing a huge role in his success. Says Raymond, "I'm a Facebook guy, following friends and family. The niece of a close friend designed my web page, did our social media and it was *very* effective. One of his grass roots efforts included orange t-shirts. Dozens of kids wore them. It went viral and was critical for the election victory.

"One thing I learned is the importance of staying in touch." Raymond now uses social media to share his personal story and talk about current initiatives. "It's not about me, it's about the position and what we are doing about it. I'm learning to wear the badge, it's my role and I'm honored to represent Hermosa Beach, but it's not about me."

THE SHOW MUST GO ON - MJ PEDONE

Having produced or participated in over 1,000 charitable events, no one knows better than MJ Pedone the importance of giving back. It started from a young age, as my parents were very philanthropic. We volunteered at soup kitchens, donated to many non-profit organizations, attended charity events as a family and my father even invited homeless individuals over for a meal."

Coming from the modeling world, MJ knew she wanted to do something in sports and philanthropy. Many athletes and celebrities didn't know where to start. Her firm specializes in forming a non-profit, helping them get exposure, and catapulting the endeavor.

One of MJ's strategies has proven successful time and time again. With each event, she helps create an Ambassador's Circle and utilizes high-level executives to bring more credibility to the event. With her vast network of relationships, this can be done simply through a few phone calls. "Your network is your net worth. Properly managed, it's always there to assist in your goals while helping each with theirs."

THE SOCIAL BANKER - JOSH FOLDS

After twenty-seven years in the industry, Josh has seen it all. Watching social media become more and more integrated in our daily lives, he knew that it was time for the banking sector to up its game.

Since 2010, this social banker has built an impressive community on LinkedIn. With over 23,000 followers, he's now teaching bankers around the country how to utilize this powerful tool. "Some banks have caught on, and many spend over a million dollars a year on LinkedIn."

Josh is quick to point out that only a few hundred of his relationships drive core business. He's also transitioned to do more speaking and educating. Building a course from scratch, he created a 30-page "go to" guide helping others establish themselves via social media (LinkedIn). "It's a true game changer for the next generation. Diversification of new business comes more from the virtual space. It's been very successful. It's the primary driver."

On LinkedIn, groups can be customized per business vertical (health care, business owners, etc.) His bank also helps clients utilize this tool to sell their own services. "It's now a prerequisite part of their business day. Too many get hung up with content, but don't understand the target market. Our employees are encouraged to build their network with current clients, prospects and other strategic relationships."

THE SPORT OF BUSINESS - TRACY DEFORGE

As a D1 athlete in college, Tracy has learned and understood the importance of networking. As soon as she began law school, she relied on this skill set to land her first job in sports when she graduated." I started talking to the right people the day I got there."

Not one to sit back and let things happen, she started the sports and entertainment law society on campus and ran the Sports Law Symposium. It provided access to many executives outside of the school and led Tracy to work at the NHL right out of law school.

"Networking is a skill and can be useful for everything," says Tracy. And she learned many professional athletes were lacking in opportunity to do so. With that in mind, The Players Impact launched their event platform. "When we put together our first in-person event, it was unbelievable how the excitement and interactions took place!" TPI is the leading, most diverse, dedicated community, known for uplifting athletes and entertainers with trusted resources and partnerships to succeed during and after their careers.

"The key to moving forward is the great balance of technology and opportunities TPI offers." Tracy is taking things international, launching Australia this spring. "Our organization now boasts over 600 athlete members." And for Tracy, the focus will always be on how to help each in their journey, get to the next level, and find ways to support the community overall.

THE STRATEGIC PARTNER - JERRY CONTI

After fifteen years of working in his family's Construction business, Jerry soon realized that his passions lay elsewhere. He found his way out through network marketing and strategic partnerships.

Driven purely by conversations, Jerry was a success in the industry. "I built a downline of over 12,000 reps. It was ALL networking. The more people I met, the more success I had."

His success continued, and soon Jerry was a company owner specializing in training. "We offered a platform for authors, trainers and speakers to connect. Our company helped to form over 1,000 partnerships and joint ventures."

"I can match person A to person B, and I have an innate gift to see the synergy to collaborate and not to compete. Because I'm more in the back office, the frequency of these partnerships decreases. But the overall value has increased."

Masterminds now play a crucial role in his business journey. He gains knowledge from the groups' diversity, the shared best practices, and the collaborative opportunities presented. Jerry knows that one of the secrets to success is learning from those before him. "It's a true shortcut to success., allowing time compression."

THE SUSTAINABILITY NETWORKER - ENZO DI TARANTO

Very few get to travel the globe as Enzo does! As a diplomat and senior United Nations official, Enzo has lived in peculiar countries like Haiti, Kosovo and Nicaragua. but also performed on world-class stages in Cannes and Hollywood. "My profession gave me the privilege to explore the planet, understand the depth of human nature and build an extraordinary network of people worldwide. Pick a country, and I can most likely make you an introduction of relevance."

Since 2018, Enzo has shifted his focus to attract politicians, bankers, luxury Real Estate developers, Yacht-makers, Fashion designers, media personalities and celebrities in CIRCLE X "The Green Trillion Club," an elite network engaged on Sustainability and Climate Finance at the horizon 2030. In addition to regular digital interaction, CIRCLE X members attend exclusive edutainment activities - combining Education and Entertainment - during major media events worldwide, from Film Festivals to Fashion and Art Weeks, United Nations Summits, and Formula 1 Grand Prix.

"To me, networking has a deep human value, but it must also be instrumental to generate profitable business, particularly sustainable business." Enzo said. "Technology expedites the development of communities, so that we can focus more on the quality of the persons, ideas, relationships and outcomes."

THE TOOL BOX - KOFI DOUHADJI

Born in Togo, West Africa, Kofi learned quickly that relationships were everything and often the *only* thing of importance in his country. "My upbringing helped me a lot, as I learned to invest time into relationships."

Graduating from college as a civil engineer, he utilized his network and expanded it to South Sudan where his company helped build a road. Now a US citizen and active-duty military, Kofi is seeing the power of his early life lessons. "My perspective on life is that it's a whole, a musical piece. I believe in harmony and follow a framework that was created internally. Paying it forward means everything."

In the states, Kofi keeps to his life lessons. Long-term relationships mean the most, and he always chooses people over profit. As his grandmother used to say, "They are worth more than diamonds."

Continuing to expand his skills, the focus has moved to social media. Accumulating nearly 50,000 followers on Facebook (by being vulnerable and sharing his story), Kofi has been able to identify new opportunities. "Over time when you master something, and it's going well, you tend to use it. When you know how to use a hammer, you treat everything as a nail."

Because of this, he decided it was time to expand his toolbox, and this led to a new focus on LinkedIn. A post from The Outlier Project caught his eye. He was drawn in by the topic discussed and comments made. Seeing it was an organization open to new members, Kofi immediately joined. "Some of the members started to purchase items from my company, and it's led to a swell of new business. I had no expectation/idea this would happen." Now that's how you use a toolbox!

THIS IS HOW YOU DO IT - MONICA AUSTIN

A true Millennial, Monica has always embraced social media. Learning early on that what you post says who you are, she's been careful with the content. "If you post it, someone will see it. That becomes your brand."

The college years provided her first real-world exposure to networking. She was taught that if you wanted to get a job in your focus industry, then you had to meet the right people. Once Monica knew who that person was, then her natural instincts kicked in, and the conversations came easier.

Now in the sports betting industry, she logs on to LinkedIn daily. It's a great place to see what her network is doing, follow select influencers, and stay on top of industry updates. To fill the gaps, Monica uses Twitter for additional news.

For daily contact, text is the preferred method, with nearly 90% of her relationship communicating this way, the rest is personal interaction. "Networking is not just professional, but every day. I'm constantly seeking ways to get into the right rooms and meet the right people."

QUOTES

"A relationship built over ten years, should not be handed over from a ten-minute conversation." - *David Homan*

"Be the kind of connector people want to be with." - *Brandon Gutman*

"All my life, I was building relationships for business. I just didn't know it." - *Scott Buss*

"Don't keep score. Sometimes it's just about getting to know people." - *Drew Sheinman*

"Every month, I take all my contacts and spreadsheet them. Never matters what CRM system I choose to use. Looking to elevate my game and stay in very close contact with my top 50 people. Not everyone is going to be able to help drive business." - *Elisabeth Flach*

"Go outside your box. Ultimately, networking is relationship building." - *Ian O'Donnell*

Here is an exercise that Danny does at the end of every year. "My Magic 100 circle is a select list of the Top 100 people I aim to stay engaged with frequently. This is supported by an Excel document and backed with deep details." Pick the people who occupy an expertise, a space, a skill set, and those who share your values. - *Danny Hughes*

"In my early days, I read the book, now I work directly with the author. It gives me the speed of access." - **Jerry Conit**

"It was just who you knew. I was an entry-level worker in the racing industry. My boss knew everyone in PR, and that's where I wanted to go. She was my 'networker' and helped me to get my first job with a premier race team. It ACCELERATED my network at an amazing speed." -**JR Rhodes**

"It's said that we become the arithmetic average of those with whom we spend the most time . . . choose your business associates and friends aspirationally in terms of their energy, intellect, character, etc." - **Todd E. Benson**

"My first lesson in college was learning that your network can influence where you land. It helped me land my first job." - **Al Reynolds**

"Some of the people that are most important to me are nowhere close to me." - **Fred Bean**

"Technology will never replace a personal connection." - **Rob and Keri**

"The basis of networking today is in person, on phone, email, media, social. There has never been a greater opportunity. It's the simplified version of communicating to build a community. If you have an open mind, and are willing to help/be helped, then we will do great things together." - **Dave Meltzer**

"The quality of my network determines the caliber of my net-worth." - **Enzo di Taranto**

"When people don't network well, they always complain." - **Hany Syed**

"You will know in less than 15 minutes if you want to have another conversation with someone." - **Kiana Laurin**

CHAPTER EIGHT

"It's remarkable to me how few people follow up after an introduction is made. Stand out from others and garner the opportunity to ask for future favors, just by doing this simple activity." *-Todd E. Benson*

TIME IS CURRENCY - STACI LATOISON

Looking back, Staci is still in awe of the kind gesture once made by a friend's mother who championed her internship at Texaco. As a young, single mother, she had no idea of what lay in store. But with the help of this family relationship, Staci secured the Bill and Melinda Gates Millennium Scholarship to the University of Houston, and then proceeded to have a prosperous 22-year career in the oil industry with Chevron including expat assignments in China and Angola.

Much like her first chapter, the second is just as amazing. Attending the Hispanic Association on Corporate Responsibility (HACR) conference during the Pandemic, she was moved by some of the speakers. "It changed everything and opened my eyes to board positions, public speaking, and intriguing career opportunities. And because of that, I started connecting with people outside of my company."

Staci decided to pursue a career in venture capital after hearing Serena Williams discuss the inequities women and underrepresented founders face in accessing capital. "I knew it was my calling in life! My skills while at Chevron prepared me for this." She soon enrolled in the Columbia Business School Venture Capital and Private Equity Senior Executive Program, and the rest is history. The Columbia University coursework and maximizing network connections allowed her direct and trusted access in becoming both a Limited Partner in tech funds and an investor in startups.

The momentum has been astounding. "Locally, I have built strong relationships with the tech community and joined the

Houston Women's Investment Group, a powerful organization of CEO's, judges, and state reps. All I need to do is send a message to one of our chat groups, and I'll gain immediate access ... no matter what the business topic."

TIME KEEPS TICKING AWAY - DAME DIDI WONG

Coming out of a Royal Boarding School in England, Didi's life was on the right path. Even though she wasn't an academic, Didi knew how to strengthen her relationships by being authentic and having an open personality.

Early on she had world-class work experiences with Vera Wang, New York City Ballet, became the face of a recognized photo studio, and spent her nights networking with top photographers in fashion, actors and celebrities. Through a chance meeting on Broadway, Didi met her husband. He was a known American actor, and his career led them to Los Angeles. Then life took a pause. The couple had four children. Her attention soon shifted to the family.

A dream, and a journey to a conference in Hong Kong, led Didi to her true passion...being an entrepreneur. She launched a yoga clothing brand, and it soon dominated the market. She traveled the world.

"I only began my journey of building my networks six years ago. Most cannot believe how quickly I skyrocketed my career. It looks like I have been working on it for 25 years." Truly a poster child for how you apply authenticity with skills, Didi is a true example of success.

"My network grew so fast during Covid, and now I am forced to set boundaries," She says, "It's not always who you know, it's who knows you. The tables have turned."

"It's all about time freedom and surrounding yourself with the right network." Such an important ideology, she hired a top executive to be her mentor. "Now I have a signature keynote speech to teach people how important it is to have the right network around you."

TIMING IS EVERYTHING - MIKE CHAFFIN

A seasoned entrepreneur, Mike's business footprint extends across business, music and politics. A random meeting at a college buddy's office started it all. "While meeting, a good friend called with a business issue. It turned out that my expertise could help, and I was immediately introduced." Now almost 20 years later, the partnership remains strong.

Like many of us, he's constantly approached. "If someone connects to me randomly, I tend not to pay attention. I like to follow the networking process and appreciate relationship introductions."

For Mike, tenacity can pay off. So can a well-placed message. "Most people will drop off after five or six tries, and not think about how much of my time they are wasting. One prospect was contacting me twice a week, then wasn't ready for the call when I took it. He didn't have his stuff together."

Some of his best tips are below:

- It's a balancing act to build and manage relationships.
- I have always been empathetic to take meetings and calls when I can. "That one call, that one visit, that one message can make all the difference."
- Busy does not equal productivity. You can load up your calls with activity, but often no results come out of it.
- Credibility and connection can come with certain organizations.
- Luck had everything to do with it. Put yourself in the right position.
- The message is as important as the approach.
- Time is our biggest asset. If it's wasted, you can get caught out of the network. Valid business reasons help to keep your name at the top of the list.

TOP OF THE PYRAMID - LAUREN WALSH

Once a "flyer" for the Purdue University cheer team, Lauren has seen it all. As a collegiate athlete she had a great vantage point to truly understand what the players were experiencing.

"I had a different perspective, because I lived it, and because I knew the players as humans, not just athletes."

Never shying away from a challenge, Lauren decided to work in the sports industry. Her initial plan was to be a stylist for some of her friends that were getting drafted into the NFL. But entering this vertical proved to be anything but easy. "I showed up everywhere, paid to get in the door and maxed my resources." She continued to push, making cold calls, sending emails and just being there.

Going to the NFL Combine, she realized how easy it was to walk in the door (wouldn't know that without doing it). Little conversations eventually led to opportunities. "I started setting up meetings because I knew I would be there. One sports agent I invited every year for coffee and got turned down. But eventually he recommended me to a star NBA player."

She also carefully follows social media and commercials for business, and not entertainment. "It allows me to see what they are posting and who they are talking about. It's a conversation starter when I hear of a brand that's on a podcast or in a commercial. This gives me great information to negotiate on behalf of my clients."

These days Lauren does most of her deals from relationships created, or by leveraging other access she's created. "I'm continually speaking to all relevant brands, and now network at peer-to-peer level (Executive, C-level). You never know how long someone will be at a brand. People don't stay at the same company forever. When they move on, I can garner new business."

Staying in touch on a personal level creates professional opportunities, and this is easily done through social media. Lauren uses a spreadsheet of her contacts organized by cities. "When on trips, I'll make sure that I can see everyone in the market I'm visiting."

WALL OF FAME - CINDY SISSON

Many speak it, but few live it. Cindy is one of those rare Super Connectors. From her first job in the mid-'80s, she always strived to find common ground and make introductions. "I like it because I can help people with their dreams. It's the gift God gave me. The beauty is that I don't expect anything in return."

Her "Bathroom Wall" is a legend amongst her friends. Says Cindy, "It came from a dream. I started sorting out my business cards. The ones that caught my eye went above it (the toilet); all others went to the bottom, with over 4,000 cards covering the walls." She eventually sold the house, and the cards stayed behind. "This time, I'm going to use plexiglass, so it's moveable."

"The best trick to networking is LinkedIn," says Cindy. "There is nothing else that I have found better, and I have generated tons of business." She's amassed over 10,000 followers and carefully manages them to maximize results. "I'm not trying to grow my network right now, but try to downsize so I can better deliver what I'm working on."

Cindy has now turned her attention to Motor Sports and networking with senior-level executives with the non-profit Women in Motorsports North America, a community of professionals devoted to enabling opportunities for women across all motorsports disciplines.

"Our signature event is Women with Drive - driven by Mobil 1, an annual industry-wide summit that brings the leaders in the motorsports industry together to advocate for women in the motorsports industry. It's all about networking." In 2022, the WWD II summit hosted 330 women and men at the Charlotte Motor Speedway. Her goal is to attract more than 1,500 on November 7/8th following the NASCAR Championship Weekend at Phoenix Raceway.

WE ARE THE WORLD - RACHEL GERROL

Always a "child of the planet" Rachel held several key roles in global organizations, including working for a U.S. Ambassador for eight years and an influential family focused on social impact.

In 2011 (The International Year of Youth), Rachel took it upon herself to write to the United Nations and propose a groundbreaking idea. Rachel wanted to bring together next-generation members of the world's most influential families to leverage their collective influence to make a difference through philanthropy. The UN said yes and gave Rachel and her co-founders six weeks to put an event together. Seventy-five young leaders showed up, representing billions in family wealth. Conversations crossed every subject area. It was a huge success and started a movement. NEXUS (www.nexusglobal.org) was born! A few months later 350 people from 50 countries joined a larger event NEXUS organized at the UN. Rachel quit her full-time job and made this her life's work.

"The idea of seeing everyone on earth to be here to help one another's dreams come true is central to how I see the world."

Rachel says, "Always lead with an offer." Through NEXUS, Rachel flipped the script on networking. She asks, "What's your passion, and how can I help?" Her advice is to lead from the heart to build trust, inspire collaboration, and show up for people by adding value to their lives.

NEXUS now spans the entire planet with chapters in 70 countries. 45 summits have been hosted, and over 6,000 members (with a net worth of $750 billion) belong to the organization, which is a non-profit that vowed never to solicit its members. Diversity is the focus, as the organization collaborates with Heads of State, First Ladies, Noble Prize Winners, and other cultural influencers. It is truly a relational network.

"Our primary communication tool is WhatsApp for member connectivity, and Signal for more confidential discussions. We organize weekly online discussions that touch on a variety of subjects. In 2022 we hosted our 10th Global Summit in NYC, in addition to organizing summits in Latin America and Australia and retreats to the US, Europe and the Middle East. This helped to make up for the pause of in-person events caused by the pandemic."

NEXUS was originally for people in their 20s and early 30s. "Our expectation was that it would be peer-driven, and that members would elect to move on as they get older. To our surprise, NEXUS turned into a lifelong journey where members continue to shape and grow, and the membership is now in their 30s and 40s. As the world evolves, so do we. NEXUS is now defined as being for social impact leaders who are young, and young at heart."

WHAT COLOR IS YOUR PARACHUTE? - POOJA IKA

It's a question most of us ask ourselves, and sometimes the answer is never found. And in today's day and age, there is unlimited access to knowledge, people and opportunity. "My generation was the one that created SnapChat. It evolved more to Instagram so we can see what people are up by observing what others post, I learn so much - like targeting audiences, and learning how to market to others."

Growing up, Pooja spent many of her weekends watching her dad talk on the phone for work.

"He would always tell me that it's easy to meet someone, but harder to stay in touch and foster a long-term relationship. I watched him reach out to others, even if it was just a quick hello. It was important for him to stay in touch with people not just when he needed them, but always, to show he valued the relationship and the people behind it. Without even realizing it, just by watching him I was picking up on valuable lessons that I would use much later in life, and it helped shape me into the person I am today."

Being observant always pays off. "I'm fortunate enough to have grown up in an environment where I was always thrown into things and learning important things. To this day, I'm still learning. It's important to continue to improve on our skill sets. I'll watch people in business verticals navigate tough conversations with clients and learn how to take a negative and turn it into a positive." Today, it's often hard to tell the difference online between business and personal.

Like many, she created both private and public-facing accounts. "When the trust level is up, the access is up. Now I can do everything on my phone. As the screens get bigger, the options get better." WhatsApp is her go-to for international business. "My networking channels are usually focused on specific business projects. It's about the quality of people, and not the quantity. Always try to build relationships across both business and personal."

WHEELS, WINGS AND WATER - JENNIFER JONES

Coming from the sports, entertainment and the yachting industry, Jennifer (AKA – JJ) has always been fiercely loyal to those that support her. But, the luxury event industry can be fraught with challenges, the naysayers have been many ... and often.

Almost six years ago at a dinner with yacht manufacturers, she noted "I'm looking to create a new luxury experience in the industry, which includes yachts, luxury cars, and personal aircraft wrapped with talented musical acts to entertain guests all weekend, What do you think?" and that was the dinner where it all began.

In this industry, like so many, relationship capital is everything. "The concept has been embraced by the marketplace, not only from the attendees, but also from the exhibitors/sponsors," Jennifer said. "Most events focus more on the gate, but we took the opposite approach and focused instead on the relationships and highly vetted attendees."

In their first year, 2,000 people came through the gate. The last event eclipsed 15,000 with each being invitation only.

In this luxury space, the challenges remain, especially for women-owned small businesses. "I started my own boat show from concept to completion, and after hosting for the past six years, the concept is being embraced globally and the company is still executing multiple events for luxury brands across the globe, beyond the show," Jennifer said.

The Steelpointe Yacht and Charter Show remains "Invite Only." Its undercurrent of networking provides an intimate opportunity for both buyers and sellers to have meaningful conversations. Key supporters receive contact year-round, opening up an even higher elevation of connecting.

"The relationships made this happen. While money and cash flow are important, the trust of the yacht manufacturers, the sponsors, and the attendees has been paramount. We are never going to change."

WHO'S YOUR OPRAH? - SCOTT MACGREGOR

"Access means everything. The person in the world with the most access wins. Period! If you were Oprah's best friend, you would....thru Oprah, have access to every human being on the planet. There's' not one person who wouldn't answer her call. Ask yourself, who are my Oprah's? I double down on those relationships more than any other. If you can't name yours, you can't strategically move forward."

WIRED IN - SETH BUECHLEY

Even after a life in the telecommunications industry, Seth knows that networking is all about the personal connections. Focused on getting past the technology, he sends a copy of his book, Ambition, to the key leaders he meets. "I didn't write the book for that reason and only wanted to tell my story. But once they have read the book, they know me at a deeper level and that accelerates our relationship."

"People are listening to your words, whether it's on a social platform, in print, or on a podcast." Seth often hears from executives, many who share their feedback on the book. "It's continued to give long past its creation. And I always hope the book keeps getting passed on so others can access the benefits of gratitude."

Now Seth is embracing the podcast space. "I didn't know if the show would be more personal or business, but I wanted to create content and meet influential people from around the world." He's seen great success, establishing many new friendships. And now he's exploring expanding into video-first content or even TV.

"There is a difference between sitting in your studio and recording a podcast vs. lights, camera, action! It's another level of energy. You can't edit live, so what you see is what you get."

Always seeking to influence others favorably, Seth continues to put himself in positions for new opportunities. "Organic interaction can provide great outcomes. I always make it a point to have unstructured time at the networking events and conferences I attend. You never know who you are going to bump into."

QUOTES

"Consider it relationship building instead of networking - focus on the other person and create a vehicle to attract suitable types." - *Mary Kurek*

"Great connectors are always thinking about the universe of opportunity that continues to expand with each new person they meet." - *Samantha Katz*

"I got tired of looking at the pile of badges on my desk from countless events last year. Too much time was spent on wasted meetings, wasted events, wasted conversations. Need to deepen current relationships and maximize the client base I have to expand my business. Don't need to grow more, need to look at each." - *Alice McLaughlin*

"If you are going to do something, do it right, do it strong, do it all. Show up to win!" - *Kenny Hazlett*

"If you have the time, the most effective networking tool is in person and in a group. Social media provides lots of exposure, but it typically doesn't bring me the face-to-face opportunity that has brought me the greatest success in cultivating a relationship." - *Howie Schwartz*

"Networking is relationship building. For people to know, like and trust you takes time." - *Jason Kolker*

"Slow down to speed up." - *Jerry Conti*

"Speed networking is not as valuable as a single conversation with a competent individual." - *Danny Hughes*

"Talk to everyone, magic happens in conversations where you least expect it." - *Carrie Nikitin*

"The only way we discover blind spots is when we spend time with people." - *Aaron Walker*

"Time is our most important commodity, and we need to use it strategically." - *Enzo di Taranto*

"Time is not money. Relationships are. You can have all the time in the world. However, without the right relationships you're not going anywhere." - *David Shteif*

"We are wasting time on things that don't make us efficient. There are times when you can have an important conversation by phone/video, instead of spending the three hours it would take to get to and host the meeting in person." - *Luciane Serifovic*

"Your energy and enthusiasm will help to attract the right people." - *Didi Wong*

CONTRIBUTORS CORNER

Aaron Walker (Nashville, Tennessee). Leads the ISI Mastermind Facilitators, coaches and serves as visionary for View from the Top (www.viewfromthetop.com)

Al Reynolds (Los Angeles, California). Principal and Chief Strategy Consultant at Champion Advisors LLC

Alan Pavlosky (San Francisco Bay Area). Owner Administrator at The Good Earth School

Alex Thompson (San Jose, Costa Rica). Founder and Chief Executive Officer Legaroo (www.legaroo.com)

Alice McLaughlin (South Florida, NYC). Founder of Classy Disruptors

Alycia Powell (New York, New York). Co-Founder of Champions for Philanthropy (www.championsforphilanthropy.org)

Amanda Hengst (Sarasota, Florida). Director of Distributions, Automation Empire

Amobi Okugo (Sacramento, California). Owner and Founder, A Frugal Athlete (www.afrugalathlete.com)

Andy Andrus (San Francisco, California). Entrepreneur, Consultant, Philanthropist

Brandon Gutman (New York, New York). Co-Founder and Co-CEO of Brand Innovators (www.brand-innovators.com)

Bridgette Bello (Greater Tampa Bay, Florida). CEO and Publisher at Tampa Bay Business and Wealth (www.tbbwmag.com)

Carrie Nikitin (United States). CEO/Board Member/Founder/Advisor/Consultant/Serial Entrepreneur

Charles Baker (New York, New York). Co-Chair, Entertainment, Sports and Media Group, Sidley (www.sidley.com)

Charles Kim (Beverly Hills, California). CEO Crave Global (www.craveglobal.com)

Chris Chaney (United States). Sport and Esports/Startup Entrepreneur/Advisor/Investor

Christina Heller (Los Angeles, California). CEO at Metastage, Inc. (www.metastage.com)

Cindy Sisson (Mooresville, North Carolina). CEO at GSEvents

Clayton Frech (Los Angeles, California). CEO, Founder and Career Coach at Ampla Institute

Cody Harvey (Indianapolis, Indiana). Co-Founder and CEO, Breakout App

Craig Handley (Portland, Maine). Songwriter, Musician, Founder at ListenTrust and SocialClose, Author of Best Selling Book, "Hired to Quit"

Daniel Puder (Miami, Ft Lauderdale area). Founder and President, Deputy Sheriff, Top 20 USA Podcaster, Pro Athlete (www.mylifemypower.org)

Dame Didi Wong (Los Angeles, California). Speaker, Investor, Producer, Entrepreneur, Mentor, Author, and Mother

Daniel Hughes (United States). Co-Founder and Partner, LOHAS Advisors.

Darrah Bruestein (Atlanta, Georgia). Founder and Coach, Mind Your Business Accelerator.

Darrin Gray (Fishers, Indiana). CMO, Athletes in Action.

David Meltzer (Irvine, California). Co-Founder of Sports1Marketing. Consultant and Business Coach. Keynote Speaker. 3x Best Selling Author.

Dave Sanderson (Charlotte, North Carolina). International Keynote Speaker

David Homan (New York, New York). Co-Founder and CEO, Orchestrated Opportunities. CEO, Orchestrated Connecting.

David Shteif (Boca Raton, Fl). Executive Vice President of Corporate Development, Digital Media Solutions Group.

Derek Champagne (Fayetteville, Arkansas). CEO of The Artist Evolution and Host of Business Leadership Series Radio Show (ESPN) Podcast.

Dhardra Blake (Palm Beach, Florida). Founder and CEO at Luxurydaycharters.com

Diane Byrne (New York City Metropolitan Area). Founder and Editor of MegayachtNews.com

Drew Sheinman (Miami, Florida). Founding Partner at Brand Velocity Group

Elisabeth Shaner-Flach (Tampa, Florida). Digital Marketing, E-Commerce, Tik Tok Ad Expert, Keynote Speaker.

Emil Luth (Copenhagen, Denmark). Cultural Catalyst, Fine Art Investments.

Enzo di Taranto (Miami, Florida). Climate Finance, Celebrity Diplomacy, Global Campaigns.

Eric W. Dahler (Palm Beach, Florida). Co-Founder, AQUARITAS Impact. Partner, Kingfisher Yachting.

Ezra Frech (Los Angeles, California). 2020 US Paralympian. Co-Founder of @angelcitysports

Fred Bean (Miami Beach, Florida). Founder and CEO, Hotelport. Travel Industry Analyst. Hospitality and Travel Tech Evangelist. Corporate Relationship Rainmaker.

Gibson Harnett (New York, New York). Business Development Manager at FEVO.

Gina Scott (Washington DC). Vice President, Group Licensing, NFL Players Association.

Greg Antonioli (Greater Boston, Massachusetts). Owner/President, First Call Residential.

Greg Santore (Cherry Hill, New Jersey). Chief Operating Officer at Vanguard Building Solutions, LLC

Greg Sidders (North Yarmouth, Maine). Pastor at White Pine Community Church.

Hany Syed (Los Angeles Metropolitan Area, California). PE/VC Professional and Founder.

Hayden Kopser (New York, New York). Co-Founder and President, North Improvement, LLC.

Howie Schwartz (New York, New York). Owner, Grandstand Sports and Memorabilia, Inc.

Ian O'Donnell (Sarasota, Florida). Enterprise Account Executive - CPG, Google Cloud Platform at Google.

India Wilkinson (Atlanta, Georgia). Owner and CEO, Mane Street Market

Isaac Reshad (New York, New York). Managing Director at Global Access Partners, LLC.

John "JR" Rhodes (Charlotte Metro, North Carolina). Brand Strategist, Revenue Generator.

Jason Ford (Frisco, Texas). President at Frisco Economic Development Corporation

Jason Kolker (Ft Lauderdale, Florida). Co-Founder at Nobody Studios.

Jason Maniecki (Tampa, Florida). President and Head Coach for All Pro Realty Network

Jeff Turk (Escazu, Costa Rica). Co-Founder, Mount Hydra Biotech

Jeff Tutor (Los Angeles, California). Managing Member, Yoduh Capital Holdings.

.Jeffrey Menaged (New York, New York). Founder and CEO at Chief Executive Air.

Jennifer Jones (Fairfied, Connecticut). Managing Partner and Co-Founder at Showpiece Shows.

Jerry Conti (Temecula, California). Chief Executive Officer, BoomSTR.

Jim Germanakos (Toronto, Canada). Retired NYC police officer

John Brenkus (United States) Founder and CEO of BrinxTV

Josh Folds (Palm Beach Gardens, Florida). Head of Small Business, Small Business Banking, Merchant Services and SBA at First Horizon Bank

Julie Schmidt Hasson (Sugar Grove, North Carolina). Founder at Chalk and Chances.

Julius Jackson (Miami Gardens, Florida). Social Impact Entrepreneur.

Ken Hubbard (Las Vegas, Nevada). Early Stage Executive Coach, Investor, Fund Manager.

Kenny Hazlett (Charlotte Metro Area, North Carolina). Senior Account Director at GMR Marketing.

Kiana Laurin (United States). Founder and Chief G.R.I.T. Officer, Gratus Connecting.

Kofi Douhadji (Papillion, Nebraska). Author, Keynote Speaker, Executive Coach, Podcaster, Entrepreneur.

Kristi Wells (Washington D.C.). Chief Executive Officer at Safe House Project, Inc.

Lauren Walsh (Chicago, Illinois). Founder and President, LW Branding.

LaVonne Idlette (Fort Lauderdale, Florida). Passionate Wealth Strategist for Athletes and Professionals.

Luciane Serifovic (New York, New York). CEO and Founder, Luxian International Realty,

MJ Pedone (New York, New York). President and Founder, Indra Public Relations.

Maayan Gordon (Birmingham, Alabama). Founder, Maayan Gordon Media.

Marc Jarrett (Horsham, England). Managing Director, Emjay Consultancy, Ltd.

Marc Sternberg (Los Angeles, California). Co-Founder at Brand Innovators, LLC.

Marissa Fayer (New York, New York). Non-profit CEO of HERhealthEQ; Medical Device CEO of DeepLook Medical; Partner at Goodess Gaia Ventures; TEDx speaker.

Mark Moyer (New York, New York). Founder, Win Again; Author - "Win Again"; Speaker, Podcast Host

Mary Kurek (Atlantic Beach, North Carolina). Founder and President, Frontrunners Development, Inc.

Matt Kowalak (United States). Director of Business Development, KaiKou CBD

Michael Goldberg (New York City Metropolitan Area). Knockout Speaker, Trainer, Coach!; Founder of THE Networking Group; 2x TEDx speaker; Author.

Michael Moore (Miami/Ft Lauderdale area, Florida). CEO, Moore and Company, P.A.

Mike Chaffin (Dallas, Ft. Worth, Texas). Co-Founder Three Commas, LLC

Monica Austin (Philadelphia, Pennsylvania). Partner Support Manager, Kambi.

Nancy May (Greater Tampa Bay Area, Florida). Governance and Board Expert; Author; Podcast Host; Caregiver Advocate; Global Advisory Board, Docusign.

Neil Hobday (London, England). Serial Entrepreneur; Advisor.

Nicole Middendorf (Greater Minneapolis-St. Paul Area, Minnesota). CEO, Prosperwell Financial.

Pooja Ika (Boston, Mass). Founder and CEO at eternalHealth.

Rachel Cohen Gerrol (Los Angeles, California). Co-Founder and CEO of Nexus.

Raymond Jackson (Hermosa Beach, California). Mayor, City of Hermosa Beach.

Rebecca Longawa (St Paul, Minnesota). Founder + President, Happy Warrior; Advisor and Mentor, Stadia Ventures.

Rob and Keri Stuart (Orlando, Florida). Co-Founders of Creating Magic Vacations.

Rob Vaka (Alpharetta, Georgia). President and Chief Revenue Officer, BrinxTV

Russell Rieger (Sea Cliff, New York). CEO and Co-Founder, CHNL Holdings, Inc.

Samantha Katz (New York, New York). Champion of Inspiring Leaders

Sasha Lund (Nicosia). Family Office Relations; Legacy Builder; Serial Entrepreneur; Podcast Host

Scott Buss (Phoenix, Arizona). Founder, Advent Jets.

Scott MacGregor (New York City Metropolitan Area). Founder and CEO of SomethingNew LLC and Founder of The Outlier Project.

Seth Buechley (Roseburg, Oregon). Owner at Cathedral; Wireless Industry Investor; Board Advisor; Author; Keynote Speaker

Shane Mahoney (Lakeland, Florida). Founder, Lugos Travel.

Shannon Leroux (Greater Toronto Area, Canada). CEO, Co-Founder SIVVA, Keynote Speaker

Sharmilla Shakti Patel (Berkeley, California). Founder and CEO at GreenTech Laboratories, Inc.

Staci Latoison (Houston, Texas). Founder and CEO, Dream Big Ventures LLC

Stacy Grant (Marsh Harbour, The Bahamas). Sales Executive at OneWater Yacht Group.

Stephen Meade (Beverly Hills, California). CEO and Founder at MonetaPro, Inc. and MagMo

Stephen Wilson (Pensacola, Florida). IP, Sports and Entertainment Attorney at Beggs and Lane, RLLP

Stephynie Malik (United States). CEO @ SMALIK Enterprises; Chairman @ MalikCo

TJ Rives (Greater Tampa Bay, Florida). Radio Broadcast Personality.

Tiffany Smith (Los Angeles, California). Owner, Rise Above Entertainment.

Tim Hayden (St Louis, Missouri). Co-Founder @ Xvisory and Stadia Ventures.

Todd Benson (New York, New York). Investor, Advisor, Board Member.

Tracy Deforge (Boston, Massachusetts). CEO and Founder of The Players Impact

ABOUT THE AUTHOR

Scott Manthorne is Founder of www.theinsidecircle.net, a private global networking organization that specializes in connecting high performing entrepreneurs and CEO's. Since 1992, his efforts have helped to move over $500 million in new sales across every continent in the world.

His diverse footprint includes a rich history in the professional sports sector where Scott launched two niche organizations (Athletes and Executives and All Sports United). AandE focused on bringing retired professional athletes closer to business. All Sports United was a think tank powering the non-profit initiatives of the world's top sports properties, organizations and athletes.

In recent years, his focus shifted into the High Net Worth Sector. Current initiatives focus within the Family Office Sector, along with Private Aviation and Yachting.

He enjoyed 12 years coaching softball and soccer and has a Black Belt in Tae Kwon Do. Scott also loves traveling globally, supporting key philanthropic initiatives, mentoring the next generation, being active (a passionate Pickleball player), and spending time with his daughter, family, and close friends.

He is often asked, "How did you learn to network?"

His response is, "I am not gifted with height, looks or athletic prowess, I leaned on my social skills to maintain peer status."

Scott's journey started in 1992. Since then, he has helped to create seven specialized networking organizations, written 100 articles, given 200 presentations, and ran more than 500 personally facilitated Conferences, Forums, Roundtables and VIP Receptions.

Like the rest of this book, I'm sharing my journey with a bunch of short stories below.

Community Service - Jaycees. From an early age, I remember going around town with my father to different gatherings hosted by the Jaycees. For those that don't remember, this was a locally based organization of young executives who did many things to support their communities. This has led to a lifelong commitment to charitable endeavors. I have served on countless boards, headed multiple fund-raising efforts, and continue to provide guidance to numerous executives and organizations in the industry.

Fraternity Life - It may sound silly, but being part of a fraternity was life changing (sounds just like the line many of us heard when pledging). Obviously, the social aspects provided more fun than I deserved. But it also taught me many important life lessons. Having to deal with alpha personalities, constant distractions, "drama" from all directions, and all the social opportunities provided amazing learning experiences. I walked away with exceptional communication skills, organizational skills, and an appreciation for how a functional network can produce results.

Martial Arts - There is a story here, and in itself a "network effect." While in college, many of us would often visit the favorite watering hole for all the college students. Over time, I became friends with the owner. What I did not know was that he was an accomplished Martial Arts Instructor and owned a school in town.

With limited athletic background, I was more than hesitant to attend a class. But after some time, and maybe even traditional "peer pressure," I attended my first class. The rest is history! After three years of training, I received my Black Belt in Tae Kwon Do. It was an achievement I will always be proud of! The achievement is truly hard to put this in words. I learned many lessons. They included discipline, humility, tenacity, drive, honor, integrity and compassion (to name a few). Not a day goes by that I don't apply what I learned to life, to business, and to those around me.

The Rainmaker - My first business exposure to networking was in 1992, and not where you would expect. Fresh out of college, and wanting to be an entrepreneur, I became part of the Amway business. "Drive the miles, show the plan." "Some will, some won't, so what." I was energized by this fascinating community. Soon, I found myself using my network to bring friends, business contacts, and anyone with an ear to presentations. Although I never succeeded financially, it was an important part of the journey.

The Story of LinkedIn - It was 2003, and 'online' networking was just starting to take form. I was at the height of my activity in this space (writing articles, hosting events, and even providing light consulting to some). One of my close friends mentioned a new website called LinkedIn to me, so I checked it out. At the time, it was in "beta" and no one in Florida was even participating.

Not knowing much more about the platform, I decided to join and create a profile. To my knowledge, I was the 2nd person in the state to join (and a very early adopter globally). As you can imagine, it did not take long for LinkedIn to gain momentum. The rest is history.

Over the years, I have utilized LinkedIn in a variety of ways; connecting to everyone I know, or don't. Following countless industry titans. Creating or joining groups. Using the platform for pure research. You name it.

LinkedIn is what you make of it. Its value is immeasurable, as no other platform will give you the immediate access that this one does. I can say without hesitation that LinkedIn changed my professional life forever. It still remains one of the most valuable tools in my networking arsenal and is always an open window on my computer. I probably visit/look at the website 20-30 times a day and will continue to do so.

Maine Move - Moving back home in 2005 to raise my daughter, I was forced to rebuild my network. Being an avid tennis player, I went immediately to the local club. The first night there, I noticed a gentleman "working the room." He went from person to person shaking hands, laughing, and receiving compliments from all. I had to meet him! We quickly became good friends, and soon after he invited me to go see a Harvard football game.

Joining us for the trip down was Steve Wilson (featured in the book), and his wife Valerie. It was the start of a long friendship where we have become close friends, served on many boards together, and traveled to 15 Super Bowl Weeks together. Steve became my attorney, and to this day has been one of the most valued friendships and business partners I have. So never underestimate that social situation. You never know what the outcome may be :)

Volunteer and School Coach - A common story for many, I enjoyed many years of youth coaching. It was not my intention to do this, and it all started when my daughter (only child) decided to play t-ball as a first grader. Being a prior Martial Arts Instructor, I guess those talents kicked in. I was soon helping to organize/run the T-ball. This led to me being asked to coach a youth softball team. I knew nothing about it, but I hesitantly agreed.

Twelve years later, I coached my final game in High School for my daughter. This was the end of a journey of hundreds of games, practices, tournaments and team activities. I also entered the coaching ranks in soccer and did that for eight years.

I'm often asked why I did it. Early on, I felt an obligation to the community, the girls, and other parents. But as the journey continued, I realized that the girls gave me so much more back. Words cannot express the lifelong effect this will have on me as I remember all the memories, see all the pictures, and continue to speak to many I coached.

Athletes and Executives - This is a story about a networking organization I built. It started in 2001, as I was entering my second year as a Financial Advisor for American Express. In that role, I had the crazy idea that it would be fun to take on professional athletes as clients. The only problem is, I didn't know any! But my years of networking taught me that there was always an answer, so I took off looking for it.

The first thing I did was attend a trade show at Tropicana Field in St. Petersburg, Florida (home of the Rays). There I met some front office employees for the team, and also the Tampa

Bay Lightning. This started my journey into professional sports. But it gets way more interesting.

Athletes and Executives was an idea born out of many things. My business partners and I knew how to create the model and had seen something similar. So, we set off to create our own networking group. The idea was to bring executives together with current and retired professional athletes who wanted to get into the business world and needed to network. And so, we began to host monthly luncheons and after-hours mixers. Soon, our organization grew to 200 participants. We knew we had something. This led to a national expansion of events, and soon the creation of an "online" community (pre-LinkedIn).

The organization went national. We expanded to 700 members. We touched every facet of professional sports. We networked online and in person. We were a success! But as LinkedIn gained strength, reach and acceptance, our business ideas became less relevant. So, in 2011 we shut down the networking community, and said goodbye to this business idea.

While the examples are numerous, I decided to share three unique examples of networking for you. Each is quite different.

Let's Make a Deal - Never in my wildest dreams did I think this could happen! It was 2019, and my private network (www. theinsidecircle.net) was continuing to grow globally. A close friend of mine regularly hosted ultra high-end events. Typically, attendees were quite wealthy, and often were treated to test drives of luxury vehicles, rides in helicopters, and tastings of premier food and spirits.

In one of our conversations, I asked how I could work with this company. An introduction was soon made to the National Sales Director, and he asked if I could help to bring new clients to the company. I said, "Sure, if you give me a car to drive" (thinking there was NO way this would ever happen. But it did! A few short weeks later, a BRAND NEW vehicle arrived at my front door and the relationship started. If not for the pandemic, I would probably still be driving this luxury vehicle. What a great example of the value one's network can deliver :)

The 7-Day Curve - As the world began to shut down from the pandemic, there was a historic scramble to locate and purchase PPE (personal protective equipment). No one knew where we were heading with this historic event. Companies, hospitals, front line workers, and governments faced a huge dilemma. How can we buy more masks, gloves, and other needed supplies to protect each other?

The situation was highly complex. To make it easy to understand, traditional supply channels had been shut down. It was now a "cash only" business, and most everything that our country needed was in China. No one knew how to find the resources. And I mean no one! From this, myself and five individuals came together. In 7 days, we used our global networks to bring together suppliers and customers, building a whole new channel of relationships. It was the most fulfilling, and most exhausting experience of my life. But... we helped to deliver the needed supplies.

A Grand Slam Weekend - One of the things I love about networking is how creative you can get to achieve a goal. During the 2017 MLB All Star Weekend in Miami, one of my clients wanted to connect closely with players from the league. So, we devised a plan. It included volunteering to build a local playground, hosting an intimate dinner, and then attending the Home Run Derby at the end.

A perfect experience happened, as we brought together select executives and nearly 60 professional baseball players. All goals were achieved. And to this day, some lasting relationships continue from this epic weekend.

ACKNOWLEDGEMENTS

It takes a village, and writing this book proved the saying. Thank you, thank you, thank you to:

To my last employer, who fired me. It led to the birth of this book.

To my editor/publisher, Michael Baes. Your patience with me was extraordinary.

To the one hundred and five friends who contributed and helped write this book with me.

To my daughter, Alexandra. My rock. My pride. My Joy. My greatest blessing.

Want to stay in touch? Drop me an email (connect@ thenetworkeffect.ai)

www.ingramcontent.com/pod-product-compliance
Lightning Source LLC
Chambersburg PA
CBHW070123030426
42335CB00016B/2250